# SELLING
# EDUCATION
## AND
# EDUCATING
# SALES

# SELLING
# EDUCATION
## AND
# EDUCATING
# SALES

TYING IT ALL TOGETHER

*A survival guide for: New teachers,
tired-tenured teachers, sales managers
and aspiring sales professionals.*

Brian L. Gross and Chuck Thokey

Archway Publishing books may be ordered
through booksellers or by contacting:

Archway Publishing
1663 Liberty Drive
Bloomington, IN 47403
www.archwaypublishing.com
1 (888) 242-5904

Because of the dynamic nature of the Internet, any web
addresses or links contained in this book may have changed
since publication and may no longer be valid. The views
expressed in this work are solely those of the author and do
not necessarily reflect the views of the publisher, and the
publisher hereby disclaims any responsibility for them.

Any people depicted in stock imagery provided by Thinkstock are
models, and such images are being used for illustrative purposes only.
Certain stock imagery © Thinkstock.

ISBN: 978-1-4808-3514-6 (sc)
ISBN: 978-1-4808-3515-3 (e)

Library of Congress Control Number: 2016912441

Print information available on the last page.

Archway Publishing rev. date: 8/24/2016

# CONTENTS

# INTRODUCTION

You may wonder why the combination of Education and Sales. The two really go hand in hand, with the simple difference being that Teachers are educating our future and Sales Professionals are educating based on future needs and wants. We all influence people, and teachers specifically are influencing young people of all cultures to have the desire to learn and work towards a bright future. The world of sales influences customers of all cultures to purchase a product or service that will better their situation, now or in the future. So when we look at the two professions, we can summarize this point by sharing words from Jack Malcolm, sales trainer, "Good salespeople do a lot of teaching, and good teachers do a lot of selling. Both professionals only succeed if their customers or pupils do—you can't be a teacher unless someone learns, and you definitely can't sell without someone buying."

As teachers, you may be thinking, "I can't believe that the authors are comparing us to a bunch of scum who lie and manipulate people out of money so they can make a few bucks." First, a very large majority of "Sales Professionals" truly are out to help and not manipulate you. They are simply here to help you make a good decision.

A true professional would not sell the product or service unless they believed deep down that it is the best solution to their customers' current/future need or want. Are we saying there aren't misguided sales people out there who are more concerned about their own wallet than yours? Absolutely not, but we encounter these folks as well. They won't be in the business very long before they realize that they either need to change their way of thinking, or move on to some other profession. Consumers are smarter today than ever before due to technology and the internet…the facts are now at everyone's fingertips.

We will be discussing and comparing a number of **"Hot Topics"** that impact both Educators and Sales Professionals. Hot Topics will begin with the Educator, and then switch over to the Sales Professional thoughts and opinions. Each Hot Topic will conclude with a **"Timeout"** tie in of either sales or education. This will seam together the idea of how "Selling Education and Educating Sales" go hand in hand.

**Additional Note to Reader:** The discussions and comparisons in "Selling Education and Educating Sales" are strictly unapologetic, opinion pieces based on our personal experiences in both the sales and education fields. The goal is to either bring you back to life in whatever field you have spent many a long year in, or assist in mentally jump starting your new, exciting and challenging endeavor.

# HOT TOPICS –
# SELLING EDUCATION

## Education Introduction by Brian

The concept of *Selling Education and Educating Sales* has been in the back of my mind for years, and thanks to a collaborative effort with Chuck, the concept has now become a viable reality. After spending over 14 years in the banking and marketing fields, and now 11 years in education, it is undeniable that sales and education are seamless partners.

No matter which side of the fence you are on, occupation wise, there can be absolutely no success without a strong belief in yourself, the organization you work for, and specifically the product you are selling. Most sales professionals and teachers do a tremendous amount of due diligence prior to going into their profession, and that initiates a desire to sell their product and strive to make a difference. Sadly, others obtain a job position strictly for the paycheck and the hopes that all will work out in the end. If you are attempting to sell a product or teach a process that you personally have no interest in at all…you will fail. At that point, you have two choices: Educate and encircle yourself with the product/subject to the point that you see and experience the relevance to both yourself and the consumer/student. Or, talk to your administrator/ supervisor and request a transfer into a position that will benefit everyone involved. You can only feign interest in something you are trying to sell for so long until the cracks in the pavement eventually show through. Finding your niche is critical.

Fortunately, I was lucky enough to find that niche by building my mathematical curriculum around my business background. Almost every avenue and process of math can be related to some form of business that impacts our students' daily lives. When I'm looking for relevance, it's usually right in front of my face. The students can not only see the immediate impact of math on their daily life, but also on the economics of their local business community. The goal is to foster business leaders and create the kind of "go-getters" that our country so desperately needs.

Throughout "Selling Education and Educating Sales", the reader will see the authors reference sales during the Education section, and education during the Sales section. I cannot stress how vital it is that everyone in both professions realizes how much we train and work in a joint effort, with very common goals. If Sales Professionals are willing to educate themselves and their clients on whatever product or service they sell, they will be successful. If Educators are willing to teach AND sell all aspects of their product to our young clients, they too will be successful.

So, teachers, the next time you enter a business and get mildly irritated by the young sales professional who is enthusiastically telling you all the highlights of the product that you came to their store to possibly buy, remember this…they are your professional peer and a product that you sell.

## 1. Mental preparation for the year to come

Summer's almost over and another school year is upon us. We as teachers are expected to skip back into the school and classroom, totally prepared and rejuvenated, with a big smile and open arms. Anyone able to accomplish that task, raise your hand. ·Pause· Not even a mild breeze came my way.

Now, the general public and particularly our government, have the common and growing misconception that teachers only teach in order to have summers off. We joke about it, but the belief is there. "They" believe that we are ALL overpaid, underworked, cry on our union reps shoulders daily, are constantly demanding raises, feel we are entitled, and basically have an unbelievably cushy job. We all know that this is, quite frankly, a pile.

Before we discuss some thoughts and ideas that could possibly make the school year a little easier, let's be realistic and look at examples of things that might be weighing on your mind as you walk into your classroom to teach. Remember, we tell our students to leave their issues at the door…can you?

*Professional and Political mental obstacles to your success*:

- You are starting the year with your 5th Principal in ten years. You have heard both pro and con gossip about this individual, but have no idea what to expect.
- You had a 4 person teaching team, and are now down to 2. Will you have to pick up another subject or even change grade levels? No one usually lets you know until about a week before school starts. No time to adjust or prepare. Who does this?
- Will I have to move rooms? A monumental and time consuming task in itself.
- Many of your incoming students (historically) are carrying such horrific baggage due to their home life, social media, and the ever changing world in general, that it should actually be a requirement to update your resume with Psychologist, Sociologist, and IT Specialist. (None of which you have had any formal, accredited training in, of course.)
- IPDP (Individual Professional Development Plan). Good lord almighty. Your certification expires this school year. In order to renew your teaching license, you still need either 3 Graduate Credit hours or at least 20 more Professional Development hours (If you read the continually revising chart correctly). Your district may or may not have enough PD's to cover the required hours, AND, they do not reimburse for college credit

hours. So, you may have to come up with at least $1000 to cover the college classes, and find the time to actually attend either live or online.

- There is a yearly threat of your school closing due to low attendance…thank you school board, poor management and lack of marketing!

- The state has made testing *so* cumbersome, involved, and impossible when it comes to covering all of the standards which MIGHT BE on the test, that actual teaching seems to be **less important** than the test itself.

- This impacts your evaluation, which changes and becomes more threating and frightening by the year. You could actually be fired for things that are totally out of your control. Where are the state representatives that claimed to be working for you when you voted for them?

- Due to low test scores, the state demands your district/school implements a selection of "programs" in order to ensure student growth. However, the only thing that appears to be growing is the bottom line of those who promote and sell these worthless, expensive, pseudo-educational programs for profit. These programs, in turn, often cause our students to fall even further behind due to everyone's stress level, and the time it takes to implement the programs (which, with no model we have to make it up as we go, taking even MORE time away from teaching).

- This now leads to the looming threat of state take over. Hmmm…letting teachers actually do what they were trained for, **TEACH**, would alleviate much of this *Ridiculousness*. (Yes, even teachers occasionally watch MTV!)

*Now, if that wasn't enough to weigh on your mind, don't we all have a home life and families?*

**Personal mental obstacles to your success:**

- Your spouse may work for a company that is moving out of state. What now?
- You have one child in college, and another heading there in two years.
- One child just got her license…Car Insurance doubled monthly. You threaten bodily harm if they get a ticket of any kind!
- The brakes are going out on your car and it needs new tires. Cost…at least $900.
- The central air conditioning unit just went out and you need $750 for repairs.
- You need to pay a company to bring down 3 dead trees in your yard before they fall and hit your house. Cost…$1250.
- You're not getting any younger (neither are others who live with you…but we'll leave that alone). Health issues are creeping up, you're insurance policy reads like an attorney's handbook, the

premiums have doubled, and who in God's name has time to go to the doctor?!?

- You have to figure out how to financially handle all of this when you haven't received an actual raise in almost 5 years. I ask everyone with a job, or even those looking for employment...would you work for a corporation that says every year that you don't deserve even a cost of living raise? I'm not trying to be insulting, but McDonald's gives more raises to their employees than the occupation we spent years and tens of thousands of dollars going to school for (and again, in order to remain "highly qualified", that education and outpouring of money must continue).

There is no doubt in my mind that most of you could double, or even triple these two lists, but I think you get the idea. We, as employees of this occupation that we know and (hopefully) love, are mentally in dire straits.

Many obstacles are political and out of your control. They roll downhill from the national (corporate) level, to the state (regional) level, to the upper echelon of your particular district (office /branch), to your school principal (manager /supervisor), and finally to you individually. However, some perceived obstacles are primarily in your head, created during "parking lot meetings" and those weekends after very stressful and thankless school weeks, and these issues are actually quite survivable.

**\*Sales Timeout:**

I give a scenario to my sales professionals in order to help them understand that having the ability to do the job is not the only thing that makes them successful. Let's turn this scenario into something that you can relate to. Your alarm clock goes off, and when you violently hit the off button, the clock flies off the table. It's now on the floor still screaming at you. You leap up and finally get it turned off just to turn around and hit your toe on the leg of the bed on your way to the bathroom. When you turn on the shower, you find out that you do not have any hot water, so you take a cold shower. When you finally get to work, your staff come in and sit down quietly (got you laughing now) and stare at you. You then hit them with YOUR morning, meaning that your attitude is about to not only ruin your day, but now it's impacting theirs. This doesn't have to happen, you can't avoid these types of mornings, but you can avoid passing your morning or other bad situations onto your students (and the rest of the world for that matter). We have that **Pre-Shot Routine** which allows us to alter our state of mind so that we can focus on what matters most going in our day. ATTITUDE! Whether it's listening to a motivational song (anything from Hans Zimmer to AC/DC), YOUTUBE a motivational video, pray, or call someone that always motivates you (now, don't throw your problems at that person, just tell them you need some positive words to help you face the day ahead). You need something that will change your state from "I can't wait to go back to bed" to "Let's make magic happen today!"

When we look at each opportunity given to a sales professional to make that sale, and I would even go so far as to say the opportunity for Educators to successfully teach a lesson, what it takes to sell the job is broken down as follows:

10% - Luck
20% - Your Skill
30% - Your Customer / Student's Attitude
40% - YOUR ATTITUDE

You may be a very skilled practitioner of what you do or the lesson you're about to teach, however if your attitude or your students attitude are less than willing to meet the needed effort, your lesson will fail to sink in. Take the temperature of your students but most importantly, "Check Yourself."

## 2. Setting up for success

Prior to your first day of school, take the time to preplan your own personal procedures/processes, and then set up your room.

Taking the time each year to write out a new checklist of procedures and expectations for **you** is invaluable. Every year something changes, albeit in the district, your specific school, or just the next class coming in your door. Using the same checklist year to year will result in something being missed and you looking a little ridiculous in front of your students or, god forbid, a parent or the administrator.

What do you expect the students to do when they first walk in the door? Will you greet and then explain to each student *every* step (for example) as to where to place their belongings and how to find their desk? Or will you have step by step directions, along with a written "Welcome!" on the board or screen? (This is my personal preference.) How will you greet and speak with the parents while managing the students at the same time? Which comes first, discussing your specific subject matter, or the school rules and procedures? And, do you present your classroom rules or the school rules first? Do you present end of day expectations and procedures at the beginning of the first day and then again at the end, or wait until the end of day so that you can walk the students through the process? These are just a few of the many questions you should ask yourself and plan for prior to the students' arrival (more about this in the upcoming **Hot Topics**).

Appropriately decorate your room. When someone walks in, it should not only represent you and your school, but your specific subject area. Display ALL of the names of your students and their job positions within their class/team (teams if you are not self-contained). Each desk should also have the names of the student assigned to it, as well as any locker/cubby and/or mailbox. If you plan to individually chart tests and/or homework, post the names of your students before they walk in the door. A blank chart means nothing without ownership. Also, if a student leaves the school or a new student arrives, adjust the charts and class lists immediately. Kids are keenly aware of their surroundings and will bring it to your attention, especially when it comes to adding the new student. Nothing can tear your heart out more than a new student coming to you and saying, "Don't you care that I'm here? Where's my name?" Be proactive. Students may act like they don't want to be in your class, and for some that may be the case. But, just seeing their name posted, gives them a sense of belonging.

Oh, a quick note regarding the display of tests and scores. I personally only display student work that earn an 80% or above. I've seen teachers post every test paper, both passing and failing. You are setting yourself and the student up for a very negative situation. Students know when they haven't done well, and they definitely don't need to have their nose rubbed in it. Before every test, I quickly review what is going to be on it, what the expectations are, and also explain that we are all human and make mistakes. You may not do well on this test, but let's figure out why, learn from it, and make progress on the next one.

Back to the original topic...One thing that drives me and other teachers up the proverbial wall is the self-gratifying shrines that some teachers display about themselves in the classroom (usually behind their desk). No one needs to see every award, certificate, license, etc....that you have earned during the course of your career. Family photos are fine, but don't get carried away. Students and parents want to see their work, not a teacher's life history. Use common sense and keep from looking so self-involved. It's ok to be proud of your professional achievements, but remember why you're there. Let students and peers know that you would not be successful without them. Show this by putting their accomplishments first.

Some teachers not only neglect to post and celebrate their student's successes in the classroom, they don't decorate at all. I've personally gone into classes during various times of the school year, and if I had not known up front what the subject matter was, I would have been lost until the lesson began (and *hopefully* then I would have figured it out). Not displaying relevant decorative or student work items means that the person in charge is either in transit (looking for the door), or has quit caring. Also, if that individual has occupied the space for over 1-2 months, and there are still stacks of boxes, I question their commitment. If I were to walk into a sales office that looked like this, I would immediately walk out. If I made a purchase today, they could easily pick up and be gone tomorrow. If this was my child's classroom, I would demand an explanation from the teacher. "Are you moving rooms, changing subject matter, leaving the district, etc....?" If the answer is not to my satisfaction, I am heading to the office to see if the administrator could provide a satisfactory response. There is a good chance that your concern will spark a conversation between the principal and teacher, which will alleviate the situation.

**\*Sales Timeout:**

The way sales professionals set up their offices or even where they sit in a prospects office or home, is to place them in a position of comfort for the prospect. This is a Sales Professional's power play. The Professional Sales person will make sure that the prospect isn't sitting directly across from them. In sales, we generally meet at the prospects office. When we get to the prospect's location we observe everything inside and out of the office and build a mental monument from these observations to use for commonality. We build rapport using what we found, in the end people buy from people they like and/or trust. *Street Buskers* (performers) call this "Mining the Mess". When performing on the streets of a large city, they engage the crowd faster when they keep it interactive. So they will "Mine the Mess" by grabbing a ladies purse and emptying it out on the ground. You could create an entire performance simply with the contents of what was in the purse. They may have hard candy, or even plant candy in the purse, and give a piece to a young child who is watching. While Mining the Mess, they build rapport with the lady as well as the crowd.

Turning this around for you, the teacher, observe your students as they come into the room each morning. What do they have on their back packs? In the lower grades they will have their favorite character, which is an easy topic to talk about, as well as the clothes they wear. Actually, anything they pull out of their bags can also be fun to turn into a class discussion or a writing activity. Remember that anything can be converted into a teachable moment, for children or adults.

## 3. Laying the groundwork

Rules, regulations, procedures, policies, etc... Although we all know that they are necessary evils, most of us dread but do, the beginning of the year "soapbox" speeches to our students.

First, we spell out the district rules. If your district has a Student Code of Conduct/Student Handbook, go through the highlights as a class (it's a read aloud/teachable opportunity on day 1!). And, don't make it sound like they are boring *you* to tears. If it doesn't come across that you are sold on the rules, why will your students absorb the information or care at all. If it looks like you are losing them, take a pause, start your lesson and come back to it tomorrow. Just be sure that all of the major points are touched upon AND both parents and students sign off that the rules were read and understood. Keep that form in each child's file. It may sound harsh, but having it can be great ammunition when needed. "Everyone read the rules, agreed with them and signed off stating they would follow the rules...and you broke them." Then lead into and describe your classroom policies and disciplinary steps.

Secondly, and this needs to occur in both your core classroom and homeroom (if you have both), you must review your specific school and classroom rules and procedures. Although the classroom is where the students are expected to learn, they must understand that it is also your office. What I suggest is that you post all of the pertinent positive AND negative action (Yes, I said the word negative... sometimes being PC is not reality) classroom rules in various locations in the room. Walk around the classroom as you discuss each posting. This will keep most of your students' attention by having to turn and watch you travel across the room. If you have a small group of students, have them stand and walk with you. Keep your part of the discussion short but to the point, and then open the forum to allow the students to ask questions or make comments. This is also a great opportunity to discuss the procedures for the hallway, restroom, specials (PE, Art, Music, etc....), lunch, arrival and dismissal. Especially in the elementary grades, if the rule is about a location outside of the classroom, such as the hallway and restroom, get everyone up and go there. Model what your expectations are and let them practice. Model and practice every day until the students have it down, however long it takes. Then, sporadically reinforce it throughout the year. Occasionally, things will fall apart for whatever reason. Although it may not seem like it at times, the students are looking to you for guidance, and will usually fall back in line when they are quickly reminded what the expectations were and are.

Now, I can hear some of the feel good theorists out there saying that the students, not the teachers, should set the rules and expectations. Ok, I've been to the meetings, read the books, and gave it a try for a few years. What I found it to be is a tremendous waste of time. If you keep the discussion open, you'll find that most of the rules all students agree upon are the ones you have posted in the first place. What you'll do is spend and waste quality teaching time "leading" the students to your common classroom policies. Basically, again, the students have a say, but the buck stops here. All I can say is do what works for you in that regard. But remember, your students' time as well as your own is valuable. Don't waste it being redundant. (My favorite line by *Robin Williams* is, "In the dictionary under redundant, it says, see redundant!")

I cannot stress how important it is to be consistent with your policies. When you have a discipline policy in place that states (for example), "If this…then this", never, ever, ever drop the "…then this". If you *waffle* and start to back pedal on your own policies, the students will see that as weakness and you will be guaranteed to lose all credibility. It's reminiscent of the parent who puts their child in "time out" at home. Then, because it can be inconvenient and time consuming to keep an eye on the child when they are placed in time out, the parent begins to only threaten, thinking that will keep the discipline in check. In time, the child will continue their negative behavior because they know a veiled threat when they hear one and realize that nothing is really going to happen to them.

Speaking as an urban school teacher, I can tell you that students not only need rules and regulations, they appreciate them. They may not tell you up front, but believe me they do! Students must know and understand that for every action, there is a reaction. Such is life. Many of my students have returned to visit over the years, and the majority of visitors were those I had to regularly keep in check. Usually, they weren't getting the direction needed at home, or were following their peers, and really appreciated the fact that someone cared enough to keep them out of trouble and harm's way.

---

**\*Sales Timeout:**

Sales people tend to be a form of "Maverick." Good Sales Managers understand that you need to put firm guidelines into place to keep everyone in line and even keep them from selling items or services the company can't produce. As Sales Managers, we also need to be consistent or we'll start hearing, "You allowed me to do it last week." Whether you're a Teacher or a Sales Manager, be careful making exceptions. Exceptions tend to become the norm! The #1 way to punish a Sales Professional is in his or her wallet. Slowing down opportunities that come their way or taking a certain amount out of their commissions as a fee for breaking the rules will work if done on a consistent basis. Explaining what the minimum performance goals are and how important it is that they stay over this line is a reminder of how to maintain and retain their job. Most importantly, explain and train on what it takes to be successful and what they must do if they plan on being a Top Rep!

Even though laying the ground rules is very important, your top sales organizations realize that rewards are more important than consequences. There needs to be ground rules for leadership also. Show appreciation and praise when staff, students, or fellow teachers do something well. Remember that humans move away from pain and towards pleasure, but we all like to have fun. Give twice the praise than any pain you give.

It takes some training, but one step further would be the ability to coach. Managers/supervisors give commands or direction. Coaches help team members or students come up with the solution on their own and reward them for doing so.

## 4. Know Your Clientele

Whether you're selling a product or simply trying to keep the attention of 30 kids for 45 minutes, you have to know who you're talking to. Remembering that **IT'S NOT ABOUT YOU** is half the battle. Knowing who you are standing in front of is the other half. Educators and Selling Professionals often use four categories to help understand:

(**First**) *Directors* - This student or customer is "straight to the point", and knows what they want. Many say these people have "A" type of personality.

(**Second**) *Socializers* - Everyone loves this person. Easy to sell and fun to talk to. A "Life of the Party" type of person. These customers often get cold feet after the sale, which is also called Buyer's Remorse. Buttoning up the sale or lesson is imperative for keeping their business and attention after the contract is signed.

(**Third**) *Relators* – A "Go with the flow" personality that can be talked into most anything. Often times these individuals are quiet and don't like conflict. They tend to be submissive.

(**Fourth**) *Thinkers* - These are your Engineers and Accountant type students/customers. When they tell you they need to think about it, they truly do. Load them with information and decide on a time when you will be meeting back up with them.

These four categories come from *Dr. Tony Alessandra's* "Platinum Rule Program". When utilizing the categories, you can and will treat people the way they desire to be treated. The Golden Rule of treating people the way you want to be treated is a good place to start. But, professionals should also live by the Platinum Rule.

Teachers…Open that cumulative student's file *before* the first day of school!

I personally do not care that the child had a few discipline issues during the previous years. They are my student now. A couple of summer months and (hopefully) parental intervention can often initiate change and maturity from school year to year.

However, the final grade card, notes from previous teachers and secretaries can be telling. They may have struggled both personally and academically due to the following examples: Moving 3 to 4 times during the school year; parents are divorcing and the student is in the middle of a custody battle; one parent is deceased and the other is in jail, leaving the student living with family members or in foster care; the family is homeless and living in a shelter; this list could unfortunately go on forever.

What you need to realize is that some students' priorities are completely different than others. This goes for students who live in the same town or in different states. How you teach a student from inner city New Jersey will probably differ from a student living in the bayous of Louisiana. And, both of those students may have moved to your city and are now next door neighbors...do you teach them the same way? You might, if you didn't do your due diligence first. Save yourself the headache.

You may be one of those teachers who require homework every night. That's great if this is a priority of both the student and their family. While *Susie* goes home to her house on the back nine of the local golf course, and has a designated homework time at the dinner table with mom (after her snack and a little family time to talk about her day), *Billy* goes home to an empty apartment. He is the oldest of 3 children in a single family home where the parent works 2nd shift and will not be home until after 9 pm. He arrives home to that empty apartment, has to make food for his younger siblings, figure out ways to keep them busy and out of trouble, prepare dinner (if food is available), and make sure everyone is cleaned up and ready for bed at the end of the day. He may even live in an area where having the light on after dark makes them a target for the occasional drive by. So, they live in the dark except for the glow of the television (which has become the babysitter for so many children over the years). While academics and family are the priority for *Susie*, day to day survival has become the priority at *Billy's* house.

*Billy* will probably need to do as much work as possible (abbreviated homework?) during the school day in order to keep up with the rest of the class. Have a conference with *both* the parent and student in order to come up with a plan, keep the parent involved and the line of communication open, will let them know that you care and are accommodating. **Most** parents will appreciate it more than you know. They are doing the best that they can and usually feel very much alone. However, be careful when initiating the conversation. Keep it professional and sell them on a customer service level. If at all possible, try not to bring conversations that you have had with their student into the equation. Keep it a fact finding mission that tells the parent they are not your only call…you just want to have a successful year with all of your students. One off-handed comment (that you usually didn't mean to say) during a phone conversation or even face to face, can turn an involved parent into an indignant nightmare that will haunt you for the rest of the year because you stepped out of line and onto their pride.

Lastly, show that you care, and are interested in them as not only a student, but as a human being. Maybe a family member is sick, having a baby, etc.… Jot a quick note on your calendar and have a "side-bar" conversation with them in a couple of days. Asking how _____ is doing, or that you hope _____ is doing ok, places you into a mental location outside of the classroom and humanizes you. Most students will put forth that little bit of extra effort for someone that they have some kind of personal relationship with.

On a side note, one way I keep communication open with my students is this. As students pass me in the hall, enter or leave the classroom, they will either give me a high five, or low five. This is a non-verbal communication stating how their day is going. High five equals "I'm having a good day". Low five equals "Things are not going well, either here or at home". Low five students know that the option of coming to see me privately to talk is there. This method also gives me an idea of why and how I should approach the student during the lesson.

**\*Sales Timeout:**

*Zig Ziglar* – "People don't care how much you know until they know how much you care!" This quote goes for customers, students, parents, other staff and quite simply anyone you interact with. Just don't be calculated with your conversations, be more spontaneous and sporadic. Adults pick up on false intentions (even when unintended) much quicker than students. However, adults still crave involvement and praise. When it comes to your customers, do your research. The style of selling a refinance mortgage, for instance, will vary from state to state (and even more internally). The rules and regulations are obviously different, but so are your clients. Sell yourself through a customer service approach. Find out their needs and priorities before you start your pitch. Don't assume the refinance is just to save money. They may have the money, but want to get out from under their current mortgage in a shorter time period because of a parent with health issues, and they are planning ahead (and willing to pay more). Know your area, the market, and again, your client.

*People buy from people they like (and TRUST)* Again, when we go into a selling situation or start working on a relationship to make a future sale, a sales professional understands that they need to first "Make a Friend." By earning a certain amount of trust, they are attempting to find some common ground, such as people they may know, hobbies and interests, or certain specific situations. You as a teacher need to get to know your students. By giving them a simple, and fun, questionnaire asking them about themselves and their interests, will allow you to get to know them better and give you the opportunity to work that information into your day.

You may have students that play a sport, but you should not feel obligated to go to every one of their games. However, you better show up to a couple of them in order to not only show your interest in the sport, but to also get on that personal level with both student and their parents. Quite simply, show you care and that YOU are interested in THEM and their achievements outside of school!

## 5. Transitions (for you and your students/staff)

Transitions can mean a variety of different things, but I am going to focus on the transition from class to class, subject to subject within the same classroom, and basic student movement in the room during core class periods.

Transitioning from room to room can sometimes be daunting. Go back to your day one rules. How do we leave our desk, line up and move out? As an elementary teacher, I like the 1, 2, 3 method. 1...Gather your belongings and prepare for the next class. 2…Stand and push in your chair. 3…Line up at the door. Since I set up my class in groups, I often make a game out of lining up. Whether it is the group which has the most correct answers to an exit question, or something as simple as the quietest group wins, kids love a challenge no matter what the age. Personally, I prefer to line up students in the room and transition when the other teachers are ready. Sending younger students into the hallway to line up outside of their next class begs for excessive, disruptive noise and unpredictable issues to arise. This puts you into a disciplinary situation that did not need to happen.

If you are a teacher who is either self-contained, or teaches 2 core subjects such as Math and Science (which is such a cliché why not Math and Social Studies? Marry the hands-on with the readable subject. It works!), you might struggle when moving from subject to subject. Set a time limit for each subject and, if at all possible, **stick to it**. Give approx. 5 minutes for students to finish the work for the first subject, have the objectives for the second subject posted for those eager learners who like to move ahead, and move on. Whenever possible, scaffold from one subject to the next. For example, if you are teaching a math procedure, open the social studies lesson with various types of counters used by early American Indian tribes. Make it relevant (we'll discuss more about relevance later). Students will appreciate and understand both topics when they see how they interconnect and affect their everyday lives.

On day one, you as the teacher have absolutely no idea who can work with whom, who can handle even the simplest task of getting up and walking across the room, and what students completely "get it" and will be nothing less than perfect for the entire year. I suggest the KISS method (**K**eep **I**t **S**imple **S**tupid...which is not meant to be insulting to your students. But, in this day and age of bleeding hearts and parental lawsuits, keep this as a *mental* method!). Until you get to know your class (see *Selling Education* **Hot Topic** #3), keep movement at a minimum. If a student needs to sharpen their pencil, have sharpened pencils at the ready to swap out. It's a simple raise of the hand. When students have completed their work, you can either pick the paperwork up, or have "buckets" at the end of each row for the students to pass paperwork down to. Assign one student weekly to pass out papers, etc.... Too much movement is distracting to everyone involved and leads to unnecessary discipline problems. Once you get to know your students, it is much easier to group them by both personality and academics. This, in turn, will allow more movement, such as timed learning centers and stations.

**\*Sales Timeout:**

You may be surprised, but similar to your classrooms, adults tend to act the same way in certain situations. They daydream, look at their phone or tablet when you're talking to them, and even talk to each other when you're trying to train them on something new. So, when we're transitioning to a new subject during a sales meeting or transitioning from customer to customer or phone call to phone call, it takes discipline, engagement, forward movement and most of all organization, which is something many sales professionals lack and need guidance on.

Let's start with "organization", due to its' difficulty. Organization during transition is so important because it works alongside time management. Just like a teachers' need to get the students transitioned on time so that they have a specific amount of time to absorb the next lesson, or for Sales Reps to prepare for their next client. Having a system is imperative here, and is something duplicable through other classes or clients and even in your personal life.

Any time you want someone to do something, and do it quickly and efficiently, you need to get them "engaged". Kids like to have fun just like sales professionals, so *momentum* can also play into your favor. I'm sure many teachers have taught Newton's first law of motion: Objects in motion tend to stay in motion and objects at rest tend to stay at rest. So, if you can get them engaged in the new subject, or even entering a new classroom, they will continue their *forward movement* as long as you keep leading them in that direction.

"Discipline" is going to be more on your part. Kids don't become disciplined naturally, neither do sales professionals. Putting a set of blinders on the student or sales person through expectations and observations will help them to develop a more disciplined behavior to eventually do it on their own.

*"Inspect what you Expect, because everyone is Suspect",* is another quote that is passed around throughout sales managers. Let everyone know what your expectations are during the transition, then make sure that you observe/inspect what is going on in order to insure they are doing it the way it was explained.

## 6. Become Educated *And Believe In Your Product*

Ok, most people will think this to be a no-brainer, because of the schooling we receive and the follow-up training we attend in order to retain our certification. However, after years in the profession, many teachers just start going through the motions of obtaining college credits or PD hours, instead of looking at the training as meaningful ways to stimulate yourself and your students. Whatever your core subject is, you must regularly sell yourself on your product in order to present and sell it to your students and parents.

I firmly believe that if I spend 5+ hours reading a book on my core subject (which happens to be mathematics), or spend a day at a convention or professional development class, and I pick up on *ONE* thing that excites me and will hopefully excite my students...it was worth every minute and dime. I wish the same for you as you read *Selling Education and Educating Sales*. Some of the information may seem obvious, but we are human and all need to be reminded of why we do **what we do** every once in a while.

No matter the age, students can "smell" indifference from their teacher. If you are teaching correctly and with vigor, you are exhausted by the end of each day, especially those of us who teach the same subject 3-4 times or more in the same day. It gets repetitive, and it's hard to keep the same energy class after class. But remember, those students did not put the class schedule together. The class at the end of your day deserves as much attention, excitement and respect for the subject as your first class (of whom you may have had to use a cattle prod and a song and dance to keep awake in the early morning hours of the school day!).

Another part of your continuing education is collaboration with your peers. (See *Selling Education* **Hot Topic** #7)

> **\*Sales Timeout:**
>
> You can't sell something you know nothing about. A sales person sells a product where a consultant educates you on your options and shows you how he/she can solve your problem or meet your needs with what they have to offer. "People hate to be SOLD but love to BUY!" The best sales professionals truly believe they work for the best company, selling the best product. Besides, who wants to sell the second best product?
>
> Towards the end of *Selling Education and Educating Sales*, you will see "The Ten Disciplines of a Successful Teacher/ Sales Professional." Notice #10, Belief – Having a Belief in Yourself, Your Students, Your School and Your Effort. Your self-worth and self-esteem is just as important as your students. Speed of the Leader, Speed of the Gang!

## 7. Working with Peers/Partnerships

I tell my students on a daily basis that they learn more from their peers than they do from me, which is why group work is a must. There are always nay sayers, but as I watch groups working together after a particularly involved lesson, it's amazing to see kids take up leadership roles and help the members of their group who may be struggling. This, in turn, reinforces and increases their base knowledge by becoming the "teacher". I don't care if you are a first year teacher, or on the last leg of your professional journey, watching that situation evolve is a joy to watch and will send you home with a skip in your step!

On the first day of school, I tell my students a hard but honest fact about working with either a group or partner. I'm not asking you to love or even become friends with the person or persons you are working with. We all have a job to do when it comes to teaching and learning. You must put personal feelings, insecurities, animosities, and pettiness aside when assigned a task. (I then ask how many of the students go home with anyone in the class. The answer should be none if the class lists were put together correctly...separate siblings for your and their sake!) Again, you have a job to do. Occasionally, you might discover that the person you're working with has just as much to say and contribute as you. If you feel so inclined, politely tell them that or just mentally file it away for the next time a partner or group is required. It might just sway your opinion as to who you want to work with.

The same goes for teachers and working with your peers. I keep saying this, but we are all human. You cannot and will not work in any building or corporation and "like" everyone you work with. It is impossible. But, we have a job to do. Don't let the same thing I tell my students get in the way of your success as an adult and educator. The individual who can basically drive you nuts at work, or the one that you barely see, can actually come through for you in the end. I remember a teacher that worked down the hallway from me for about 2 years. Honestly, I thought she was arrogant, conceited, and listened to nothing that I told her. But, due to my upbringing, every time we passed in the hall and made eye contact, I said hello and asked how she was doing. Being the building Tech at the time, I had also assisted her with some technology issues. But, I never thought twice about our interchanges. Then, during an opening day staff meeting, this same individual divulged to our group of peers how much she appreciated me due to my friendly attitude, making her feel welcome, and my willingness to assist her when she had an issue in the classroom. Here is a person that I really never had the opportunity to work side by side with professionally, but apparently I had made an unconscious impact on her by just recognizing she was part of our team. This really woke me up when it came to how we should all treat and respect our fellow workers.

We all hear about the importance of collaboration with your fellow teachers, but *how* we collaborate is the difference. So often we attend some type of professional development, either within the district or our specific school, and are asked to split into groups. What happens? The groups are either familiar cliques, or all of the teachers in a particular grade level. Yes, as a grade level group you have a commonality, but other than discussing or "dissing" the students that you all know, what are you going to gain from it? What is needed, and should be required, are weekly or bi-weekly core subject meetings. As a 5th grade teacher, I need to know from the teachers below and above me how to prepare for the upcoming class of students and how to prepare the students I have now for the next grade. This only comes from conversation and data. We want our students to be prepared to move on, but teachers need preparation as much as they do. Collaboration is the key. During your meetings, talk about not only the positives, but the negatives. Teachers never want to admit their failures, but why tell your students that's how we learn if you're not willing to do it yourself! I've always said that teachers are the most giving group of "thieves" in the corporate world. But, that's not a bad thing. Anything you can glean from another teacher that is advantageous for your students is nothing less than a victory in the classroom. Education is probably the only occupation where theft is allowed, and encouraged! Make it your own, make it relevant, and shoot for success.

**\*Sales Timeout:**

Success isn't achieved on your own. The relationships you build in the community will bring you more opportunity to succeed. The late Zig Ziglar's most famous quote, "Help enough people get what they want and they will help you get what you want".

\*Go forward and look at *Educating Sales,* **Hot Topic** #3, regarding *Accountibilibuddy.*

## 8. Relevance

How many of us have said, "I hate teaching ____ because the kids couldn't care less about it."? Ok, so my question is, how are you presenting your core subject? If you are teaching percentages to a group of students who have never been in a decent restaurant before, and you use the example of "tipping", how are they going to relate? First, explain how most waiters and waitresses are compensated, which is usually a low hourly wage plus customer tips. The common tip is at least 10 to 15%, but could be more or less when it comes to the customer service and the quality of the food (which unfortunately is out of their control). Then, hand the students a variety of menus. Allot a specific amount of money for each student to spend, and have them choose a variety of combinations of food (appetizer, drink, entrée and dessert). Next, utilizing their learned knowledge of multiplication of decimals, have them calculate various tip amounts (ex. Meal cost = $21.75, 15% tip = $3.26, Total meal cost = $25.01). Finally, call a local restaurant, talk to the manager, and see if you can arrange a lunch or dinner field trip. This way the students can see the wait staff in action, and put their new found knowledge to work in choosing and calculating an appropriate tip.

Keeping the subject matter relevant is not always easy, depending on your resources, but it can make your lessons much more engaging and discussion worthy. And, since most of your students will have a variety of life experiences (even in the elementary grades), this will open up student led discussions that your lesson plan never would have addressed in writing. If they are wrapping the content of the lesson into their group discussions, no matter what the core subject, you may have just hit a homerun!

Also, it takes more than pictures in a book to bring out the relevance of a topic. With all of technology available, it is almost impossible not to find interactive websites or programs that will enhance your lesson and bring it closer to home. Do your due diligence, even if you have limited resources, and field trips are difficult to push through due to monetary constraints.

**\*Sales Timeout:**

Relevance in sales is just as critical, and goes along with knowing your clientele, before you begin your sales pitch. Whatever you're selling has to be meaningful to the client. For example, if you are in the business of telemarking phone sales for windows and siding, you need to research the area you are calling before picking up the phone. Nothing is more embarrassing than pitching new windows to someone who rents their home. It's also an incredible waste of both your and their time. If you're quick on your "feet", ask for the name of the owner or landlord. This might help you save a little bit of face and keep the call credible before you hang up.

Get the product in their hands! Have you walked through the mall and had one of the skin care kiosks try and smear lotion on your hands? Or maybe you've had a home improvement company come out to give you an estimate and the sales rep puts products into your hands to perceive ownership or *relevance* of how great it would be to own the product?

Great Sales professionals create ownership of the product so the prospective customer gets emotionally involved. Same goes with your students. Make the subject of the day relevant to the student. The kids may think with their heads, but they commit to the lesson with their hearts (emotionally).

## 9. Managerial Support

Your administrator is there to support you, whether they want to admit it or not. Without well trained and supported staff, results of any kind are not going hit the marks they are striving for. Don't wait on your Principal or other support staff to come to you. Within the first week of school, set up a time to meet with them and discuss your needs, the needs of your classroom, students, parents, peers, the school, and finally the needs of the administration. Make it clear that you are more than willing to support them with school policy and procedures, but are expecting the same support in return. As important as it is for the manager to show their care and concern for the staff, it is equally important for the staff to show the same for their boss.

Occasionally, as you stop by the office to drop off some paperwork or pick up that last ream of paper, poke your head in the door of the administrator's office and just say, "Hi. How's it going?" Or, if you are in the vicinity and hear the call go out for the Principal to go to a specific room to handle a discipline issue, take a minute and meet them there. Going in before they get there and taking control of the situation might be a poor idea, for the Principal may think you are trying to step on their toes and overstep your bounds (there may be Principals that are perfectly fine with it, though. Find out quickly in the beginning of the year with either personal conversations or bring it up in a staff meeting), but be there when they arrive and show your support. The students will see the show of solidarity, and they will respect the Principal more if they see that you do, too.

Next, after you have been on the job for about a month or so, ask for feedback from both the administrator and your peers. "From your point of view, how am I doing?" "Do you see anything that I should change or need to improve upon?" Don't take any negatives personally, for they are the experienced outsiders looking in, and their opinions can be valuable. Don't worry about implementing their suggestions verbatim, but really put some thought into their suggestions and tweak your classroom/lessons appropriately. You will learn more from those "feedback request" conversations than you can imagine, and it conveys honesty, your level of commitment, and the willingness to learn to your co-workers and administrator.

Most Principals will appreciate support and dedication from their staff, however, there is always one who feels they are above it all and put up a wall between themselves and the staff. This is when you have to be dedicated and document all of your requests and conversations, which is why I keep a physical and email "CYA (Cover Your Ass)" file. Keep them dated and time stamped. If an issue arises regarding a previous conversation or correspondence, you can have the references needed at your fingerprints and squelch those pesky *he said, she said* debates and debacles.

Also, keep all correspondence and conversations politically correct. By this, I mean follow the chain of command. There is not an easier way in the world to make an enemy of your supervisor than to have a disagreement and go immediately over their head. Keep cool. Have a follow up talk (or email) and document the result. You should have a union representative in the building, so you can also have them at your side, if need be. Depending on the issue, it lets the supervisor know that you taking things seriously and want the issue resolved. If the situation is not taken care of to your satisfaction, take it to the next level. But again, follow the chain of command and be as polite as possible about it. Even if you "win" the debate, animosity can make for a very uncomfortable school year, and your students will feel it in the air.

Lastly, the principal is NOT the answer man or woman. Running to the boss to fix your problem is incredibly childlike, but unfortunately not uncommon in both education and the business world. Don't waste their time with your problems unless you have a solution in mind. This tells your boss that you have thought it through, and need either their approval or opinion before putting it into motion. They might not agree with your solution, but it opens the door for discussion and collaboration between the two of you.

**\*Sales Timeout:**

No one likes to be "managed", but most people <u>do</u> like to be coached and encouraged to hit goals and milestones. True leaders give their people room to either Fly or Fall. When someone on their team flies, those next to them are clapping and celebrating with them. However, when their team member falls, depending on the skill set and attitude of the team member, your job is to coach and mentor them into helping themselves out of the situation they put themselves in. Coach through questions and understanding while encouraging the team member to take responsibility and sell them on the solution.

## 10. Diversity/Inclusion

So many educators look upon these words as the different styles of teaching which separate the traditional students and the special needs students. In doing so, this creates the "Us and Them" mentality that can destroy a student's mental state and thusly, their academic career. With the Inclusion models, we obviously do have students who have either social or academic needs which are a distraction in the classroom. This is not the fault of the student, and therefore it is the job of both the classroom teacher and the inclusion specialist to make the necessary adjustments in order to compensate for those needs.

However, and I hope this does not offend those who teach in the special education realm, sometimes one student's needs become such a distraction that it slows or prevents teaching and learning for their classmates. This student then needs a change of venue, which may be a self-contained special education classroom or resource room. We all know that moving a special needs student out of an inclusion environment can be like going through the Spanish Inquisition, but it needs to happen...and happen quickly for all involved. Education tends to forget that teachers are responsible to teach ALL of their students, not just hit and miss while keeping their focus on that student who constantly disrupts the class due to specific needs or disabilities. And, to be fair, the same goes for the habitually disruptive traditional student. After all interventions and parental involvements have been exhausted, the same type of venue change needs to happen. This may include something as simple as a classroom change (especially for self-contained, lower grade levels), or a drastic as removal from either the building or district. We make every effort to accommodate our students (and employees), but sometimes the needs of the few DOES NOT outweigh the needs of the many.

Diversity is a term that should target *every student* in your classroom. For example, we have all had those students who are on the same academic level, but the way they handle themselves in class is night and day. One student may blow through each assignment you give them, while the other takes every given minute to complete it. However, the result for both is success. Be ready to address the needs of both. When the grade level assignment is completed by the "blow through" student, have relevant, advanced and challenging work pre-prepared for them to attempt. Trust me when I say that this style of student loves a challenge. Also, talk to the next grade level teachers. Arranging times during the week for your student to push into the next grade level and test their abilities will be a little scary for them at first, but with the permission and support of the parent, they will see it for the academic complement that it is.

As for the "slow, but steady" student, for God's sake, give them the time and space they need. Just because the student doesn't read 100 words per/minute, does not mean the comprehension isn't there. It just takes a little more time for their mental sponge to absorb the information. Have a personal space desk in the room that students can move to and away from distractions, or allow them to return and finish their work after the completion of assignments in the other classes. This could occur during Specials classes (Art, P.E., Music, etc.…), or invite them back to your room for a "working lunch". Please remember to ask permission, not forgiveness, from the other teachers before having the student return to your class.

The easy, "old school" way to handle students is to demand conformity in the classroom. Nice try...and it doesn't work. Conformity is simply the creation of a comfort level for the teacher, and has absolutely nothing to do with teaching, diversity, or the learning style of the student. What it does have everything to do with, again, is knowing your clientele. Take the time to talk to your students. What are their likes and dislikes, both in and out of the school setting? Where do they do their homework at night? In front of the TV, while talking on the phone/texting/skyping/watching YouTube, listening to music and eating dinner all at the same time? You've got a multi-tasker on your hands. Do they have academic support at home, or are they on their own? Talk to the parents/guardians and find out as much as you can about them, too. It's all relevant and impactful. Write everything down and keep it in a student specific file. This will assist you more than any standardized test data when it comes to setting up diverse, academic groups and classrooms.

When it comes to setting up "groups" in the classroom, splitting the students into low, medium, and high sections is probably the worse idea of all, but unfortunately it is often used. I prefer the low/medium/high split to be within EACH group. Peer teaching is necessary and required in my classroom. Academic groups need to discuss the lesson and any procedures before moving into the assignment. Again, I constantly tell my students that they learn more from each other than they ever do from me. If I have a group of 4 students, and 2 of the students have a reasonable understanding of the topic, after even a short discussion one or both of the other two will begin to catch on. If you don't believe it, you haven't been observing your students.

As a teacher who groups the students, your job is to teach, model, mediate and facilitate. When the students begin the group work, for all intents and purposes, they are in charge. Give them the instructions they need to succeed in the assignment, and while maintaining controls, turn them loose. It may not always go smoothly at first, but over time the hiccups will smooth out and group work will become more seamless for both the students and yourself.

Co-Teaching has become a new, but exciting trend in my district and across the nation. Co-Teaching brings the Intervention Specialist into the classroom as a teaching peer, not just the person who pulls out the students with IEP's. As a "territorial" classroom teacher, it was extremely difficult for me to allow another "alpha" teacher into my domain. I felt like this person was constantly critiquing me and my teaching style, which led to a discomfort in the classroom for everyone involved, including the students. However, the more I researched combining Co-Teaching and Inclusion, I realized that I and my students were receiving a type of reinforcement and rejuvenation that was desperately needed.

True Co-Teaching brings a second teaching style into the equation. Students now have not one, but two educators in the classroom to meet their needs. Lesson plans can be much more relevant, and meet the needs for not only IEP students, but also those yet to be identified.

The classroom teacher and students should not look at the Co-Teacher as a guest, but as an actual teacher who is there to both lead and support the students every day. Teaching responsibilities should be shared and reviewed in order to meet the needs of ALL classroom students.

**\*Sales Timeout:**

This topic is why a lot of Teachers and Police Officers make great sales professionals. Through the course of a year, Teachers will encounter and keep engaged many different types of children from every spectrum of the wealth wheel as well as the culture pallet. Teachers will also handle happy parents, overly protective parents (helicopter parents), extremely upset parents, etc.

As for Inclusion, I would dare say that this concept came from the private sector. It is true that putting slower performers/learners with peers that excel improves the performance of the slower achievers. Not wanting to be left behind is a human trait and needs to be positively encouraged. The peers set the bar and give the others a goal to shoot for. The key is having the help needed to keep the slower achieving students moving in the right direction before frustration sets in. Frustration leads to shut down and it is hard to get them moving again.

In sales teams that I have worked with, I have put the under performers with the top performers so that they can see what makes them successful first hand. Learning through observation and then doing the task on your own is the most effective way to maintain what you have learned, and learn to make it a habit towards success.

## 11. Testing / Final Results

Testing is the culminating event that obviously shows the fruit of everyone's labors. However, be smart and proactive about this process. All administrators and managers want to see progress and academic growth. I highly suggest Pre and Post testing to advertise such growth. A properly administered Pre Test lets you, the student and their parent/guardian know the child's base knowledge of the topic you are preparing to teach. Most will not do well (make sure everyone involved is aware that this is normal and not held against them grade wise), and is expected. Make it a positive by stating that this shows how much they should expect to learn in the next week or so.

As for those high achievers that do well on the Pre Test, this gives you the opportunity to really build on their advanced base and push them academically over the top. Not only should you give them advanced challenges, but a conversation should be had with the next grade level teachers. Set up days and times during the week that allows your student to spend time with a higher level class (with administrative and parent permission), and see how they handle both the academic and social challenges. Keep the parents abreast of their progress, both positive and negative, so that they know you are championing their child.

After the lesson has been taught, it's time for the Post Test. The tests can either be the exact same as the Pre Test, or similar with modifications you may have discovered were needed throughout the weeks' lesson. For those students who did not do well on the Pre Test, the amount of growth should be quite substantial (I shoot for at least 70% differences between the two tests). Be sure to celebrate not only the improved scores, but have each student chart their growth through the use of bar or line graphs. You should also chart the success and post them in the room for classmates and their parents to see. Just as companies post their earnings every month, these charts will promote how much success the students will have in your class.

New teachers...you will have one of the best days of your profession when a parent comes to you and states how happy they are to have their second or even third child with you as their teacher because of the results achieved when you taught their siblings. What a marketing tool for both you and the school!

A quick note of something that I wish was obvious. If 15% or more of the students do not perform well on a test, you must take the time to reteach. The failure was not the student's problem, it was yours. You cannot just shrug your shoulders, say, "Oh well", and move on to the next topic. Yes, we have pacing guides and deadlines, but lesson plans are a fluid creature. Sometimes you have to hit the brakes and go back. Something was missed, and moving ahead without addressing the issue will impact their ability to succeed with that next topic. Don't waste your time just regurgitating the same information in the same way either. Think of another way to explain what you taught. This will obviously help those who did not do well catch on, and give more options to those who did.

Also, if that same 15% did not do well on a test, don't shine them on to the next subject. Take the time to either meet with them individually, or in a small group in order to revisit, reteach, and/or retest the material.

**\*Sales Timeout:**

Top professionals, as well as many of the largest companies in the world, decide on what their BHAG is (Big Hairy Audacious Goal). This is the *almost* unrealistic goal that you want to shoot for. As a motivational speaker, when I talk to the kids, I talk about shooting for the moon and how it's ok to land amongst the stars. Once you have this BIG goal, your BHAG, now is the time to visualize what it would look like if you achieved this goal. Make your visualization VIVID, put the small details in the visualization. Now what are the STARS? If you were to land amongst the stars, what are those stars???

Towards the end of the month, I will start to forecast the next month. Not too long ago, my BHAG was to set a record for local roofs sold. I decided that my BHAG/Target for the following month was $2 million in sold residential roofs. I knew that the "star" was my budgeted goal of $1.8 million. I would still be happy with my team if we hit $1.8 million but WOW, the celebration we would have when we cross the finish line at $2 million + will be *amazing*. I had the whole team close their eyes during our first sales meeting of the month and visualize what it would be like to hit $2 million. What would it feel like and what would you buy to celebrate, if you are the rep that hit $300,000 in sales and takes home that large commission check at the end of the month? Take *massive action* toward our BHAG! Keeping score on each rep and making sure that everyone is working tirelessly toward their own BIG GOAL.

Lastly, humbly celebrate your accomplishment and keep from exhaling while going into the following month or semester.

## 12. Evaluations

In this day and age, evaluations are a politically necessary evil. Although they are sometimes used as modern day witch hunts on the teachers (let's admit it, some teachers need to be hunted!), they are also useful tools that can assist in planning and carrying out your lessons.

Putting aside the percentage of the evaluations which contain those pigeon-holed, state standardized tests, I welcome the walk-throughs and formal evaluations by "professional" administrators. It is easy to become complacent and sedate after teaching the same subject and grade for more than a few years. Having an outside eye looking in can make you realize even the most obvious things in your class that have been neglected, and makes you stop, think, and up your game. No matter how easy it is to do, don't take evaluations personally. The administrator is evaluating EVERY teacher in the school and, quite frankly, can become a little blinded by it all. If you disagree about something in the evaluation, take a breath, think of every possible way the conversation could go, and state your case both verbally and in writing. Just keep it professional. Evaluations can affect your career either positively or negatively, but often your reaction can make the final difference.

---

**\*Sales Timeout:**

The top Sales Managers use the *"Hank Haney Effect"* to evaluate our sales professionals. Tiger Woods holds some of the best records in golf. However he can't do it on his own. Hank Haney, Tiger's former coach, was always on the side lines watching Tiger from outside the box. Hank saw what Tiger couldn't, and then helped him to understand where he was going wrong or needed adjustment. Either a Sales manager/Senior Rep or a corporate trainer goes out with each rep once or more per month to make sure they are at peak performance. After filling out an evaluation form and identifying any short comings, we send them out with a rep that has that particular skill as strength. You will make a rep successful faster by having them watch someone do it right rather than making a list of things they do wrong and destroying their confidence.

---

## 13. Marketing

Selling yourself, your core subject and your school is actually quite an easy thing to do, but it takes a little time, effort, and money. Don't assume that the initial meeting of a parent at the beginning of the year, subsequent parent/teacher conferences, and the occasional discipline call home should be the only time you talk to them. If you really want support, show it by keeping the lines of communication open throughout the year. Make an occasional "positive" phone call home. It's a great way to build relationships, and especially for those problem students who only occasionally have a good day. Celebrate that day by calling home or even stopping by on your way home. If the atmosphere is tense in your classroom due to that particular student, imagine how it feels at home.

You also need to market your school to the community. Don't just leave it up to the Superintendent and School Board to handle this task. Few parents attend the district meetings. What they do is drive right by the school and partake in neighbor to neighbor conversations about what is going both right and wrong at their local, neighborhood school. If you have some exciting learning going on in your classroom, talk to your administrator (handle the politics) and contact your local newsroom. They are usually happy to give you a couple of minutes on their community forum. This shows that you care enough to show and broadcast what great things are happening in your school. One newscast can add 10+ students to the school roster for the upcoming school year. Side note...be sure that you have parental consent to film your students. It's an easy check, but a nightmare if you don't look into it first.

Marketing can also be achieved by your students. For example, give an assignment that has the students go to their community stores in order to inquire and survey about their current business practices. What do they sell, how many locals do they employ, what is the peak and low months during the year, etc....? Let the business owners know that the students care and are attempting to find ways to boost their sales and community involvement. Then, when all inquiries have been made and the assignment (whatever you decide to do dependent on your subject area) is completed by the students and their finding are posted in the classroom/school, invite the business owner to come to your school and tell their personal or professional story to the students. This is powerful to both students and that owner, and shows the interconnection between a school and the business community.

On an additional side note, I'd like to point out one of the most successful, yet rarely talked about styles of marketing that involved both children and parents in the 1970's and early 80's. That would be the Sunday School Church Bus Ministry. I witnessed this style of marketing as a young man while my father actively worked the Bus Ministry at various churches, but as a child I never understood the power and the impact it had on our local church and everyone involved in this particular process of divide and conquer.

One or two "personable" church members of a new church with few members (or one that was attempting to revitalize) would visit homes in the local community that obviously had children. Seeing kids playing in the front yard or a yard full of toys would raise the flag to stop. They would pass out information regarding their Sunday school program, the children's church program, and any after church or after school (during the week) activities that children were invited to attend. Now, the targets were families who were not members of any particular church, so they often were "attempting" to sleep in on Sunday morning. If you have or have had young children of your own, you know that trying to sleep in on the weekend is often no more than an "attempt", because when the kids are up, so are you. What better way to achieve that extra couple of hours of shut eye than send the young'uns' to church? The parent has a quiet house for a few hours, and the kids are building religious and moral values that will potentially follow them for the rest of their lives. Win, win!

Here is where the marketing comes into play. Churches cannot survive on faith alone; they must have parishioners who are willing to donate their time and MONEY in order to pay the bills, the pastor, and keep the doors open. So, each week a group of current church members would stop by the homes of their Bus Ministry attendees, calling this "Visitation" night.

Occasionally the door would close before a conversation could be had, but if their child has had an enjoyable and positive experience at the church, the member would be invited in for coffee and conversation. The marketing would then take a turn, scaffolding from the children to activities for the parents. Bringing the parents into the fold builds a church membership, keeps local families together and on the same spiritual path, boosts the profit margin for the church, and opens up a couple of seats on the church bus for new potential members.

I believe this to be one of the most underrated, yet powerful forms of marketing and relationship building in our social history. Schools and corporations could really learn a lesson by researching and understanding how important this could be to their school and community. Parents will not and should not send their student to a school that is not successful, or at least building their success. Would you buy a product from an unsuccessful company? Neither would I.

Another suggestion would be to talk to local marketing companies. Many would be happy to donate their services or form a community group within their company to help you spread the word about the great things happening in your particular school or entire district.

### *Sales Timeout:

Instead of talking about the types of marketing, let's talk about what marketing does and why it works. Top Sales professionals and organizations understand BOB and TOM. I'm not talking about the radio talk show; I'm actually talking about "Best of Breed" and "Top of Mind". It is imperative that we stay at the Top Of our Mind as often as possible and show you that we are the Best Of our Breed / Industry to encourage you to call. Top professionals understand that TRUST and CREDIBILITY will get you in the door and ensure a quicker sale.

## 14. Stay current

Keep up with your grading of classwork, homework and tests. Pass work back quickly, so that the grade is relevant. Change the topic of bulletin boards (both in and out of the room) at least once per/month. Never leave student work displayed for more than 2 weeks. It loses the desired impact, and parents want to see their child's progress.

Some districts require teachers to keep individual student folders. They use the work for parent conferences and send it home quarterly. As a parent, I find that to be frustrating. If my child had a test, I want to see the result. If they did well and the test was posted, fine. But, I should see the test by the time the next test is graded. Holding tests cuts down on one line of communication between yourself and the parent. Check, discuss and even challenge your school policy on student folders. It has to be best for the children and parents, not just a tool for conferences.

**\*Sales Timeout:**

Results of any kind need to be timely, especially when it comes to individual production results and evaluations. We've all been there when meetings have been postponed, maybe more than once. Doing this makes a human being feel unimportant and small. Management needs to keep to their schedule just like everyone else. This sells an employee on their value/worth to the company and will, in turn, increase production. Sales Managers grade and improve performance through "observation." Whether it's through riding with the Sales Professional all day or shadowing them at their desk, we are looking at technique and product knowledge. We aren't looking for them to make a sale at that time.

Sales Managers are watching to make sure the company's sales process is used correctly. Great Sales Managers write in a observation log and immediately (and positively) review with the employee what they did RIGHT and make suggestions in areas they didn't perform well in. We don't focus much on the short falls, as nothing will get accomplished.

## 15. Dealing with parents (Customer Service)

Both authors of *Selling Education and Educating Sales* are parents with children currently in school, and we understand the frustrations teachers can go through while working with the students. Whether it's discipline, academics or even if their child is being bullied, many parents have a difference of opinion and often decide they're going to express their feelings in person. As sales professionals, we deal with these parents every day. Below is how many of us work with such parents.

*Disarming* the parent is imperative when it comes to successfully working with them. Until they calm down enough to intelligently communicate, the conversation will go nowhere. If you decide to work with them when they are in a motivated state of anger, no good can come from it.

To disarm or calm someone, you have to listen to them intently. If they are screaming, let them scream. I know it will be hard and your blood pressure will rise the entire time they are yelling at you, but you must allow them to get out what they have to say. They have been plotting out everything they planned to say since they first found out about what ever made them angry.

Your composure is everything. Don't smile while they are lecturing you. Your face and body language should tell them you are listening and taking it all in.

Before you say a word, make sure to pause <u>4 seconds</u> in order to ensure they have gotten out everything they planned to say .4 seconds may feel like an eternity, but it is a perfect allotment of time for the parent to feel that you are listening and gives them time to either continue or even apologize because you are not retaliating immediately.

Use a "Clarifying Statement" so they know you listened and understand their complaint. (Even if you don't necessarily agree with it.) Example: "Mrs. Smith, if I hear you correctly, you feel that I have unfairly graded Jeffrey's quiz that he took on Tuesday?"

Now is **NOT** the time to start pleading your case. You want the **WHAT** and the **WHY** sitting in front of you before you give your explanation and sell them on your **WHY.** Then **CLOSE.**

The next thing you need to do is find their motivation. *"Crack the egg and find the yoke!"* Asking why they feel that way will help get to the real reason they are standing in front of you. Many teachers have experienced an angry parent because of low grades. Digging a little deeper could help you discover (for example) that the main issue is simply that their child is no longer eligible for sports. Once we find the real motivation, we can work with that and build a solution from there.

*Reversing* is another way of dealing with parents. Using the same example of a parent who decides they can argue their child's grade higher because of sports eligibility: Parent - "How is my child graded?" (STOP, don't just answer that until you know WHY they are asking, REVERSE it), Teacher - "That's a great question, why do you ask?" (You are now in control again and will find out their motivation for asking the question which may have been to paint you in a corner for an argument or strike they are about to put on you). Until you feel successful at reversing, here are some easy questions that will help you regain control of a situation or conversation:

- "That's a great question, why do you ask?"
- "You must have a good reason for saying that, do you mind if I ask what it is?"
- "How do you mean? Followed by - How do you mean exactly?"

Probably the best way to stay in the good graces of your parents is to maintain a positive relationship with their child, both during and after school. (This goes along with **Hot Topic** #4, *Know Your Clientele*.) Take a few minutes before or after school to talk or help out either academically or personally. Here's an example: Our eighth grade students were having a formal recognition ceremony after school one day. Since I taught 4th grade at the time, I planned to attend but was not personally involved in the program. A couple of my former male students came to my room because they were having issues tying their ties. I have the Windsor knot fairly mastered, so I gave them a hand. A few minutes later, here came a few more young men looking for help. As I was tying the ties around my neck and transferring them to the boys, I heard some noise in the hallway. Looking out of my door, I was shocked to see a line of young men lined up, down the hallway, and around the corner. Now, I could have gotten up, called it a day, wished them all luck, and gone home. Instead I stayed with it for about an hour and a half and made the boys presentable. What became invaluable about the situation were the conversations had with each student (how was their day, the school year, friends and home life), and the thank you calls/conversations I had with parents during and after the award ceremony. Giving up my personal time after working all day to assist the boys showed their parents that my students mean more to me than a butt in a seat and a paycheck. Since we are a uniform school, the young men were excited about dressing up, and I was equally proud of their academic accomplishments being honored that day.

If you take the time to show that you care, the "bang for your buck" is undeniable and lasts for years.

---

**\*Sales Timeout:**

**Dealing with their objections:** Again, I teach the **Four (4) C's** of working with objections. Using this when you are dealing with parents or encountering anyone that disagrees with something you said or did will enable you to handle the issue without conflict.

**Concede** - Agree with the other person by saying, I understand or I agree (Depending on what the issue is). Mrs. Smith I understand how you feel or I understand your frustration. This is meant to disarm the individual(s) you are talking to. Remember, they are looking for a fight. This is also called a *Frame Interrupt.*

**Commit** - Make the other person commit that the issue being discussed is the ONLY thing they are upset with. Do not work through one issue to find out they have a laundry list of issues they want to share with you. "Is this the only thing bothering you?"

**Convince** - Show them the facts behind your decision.

**Close** - This can be a statement as easy as "Fair enough?" or "Does that answer your question?" or "Does that help you understand what needs to happen to bring Jeffrey's grade up to a B and become eligible for sports again?".

\*At this time, be proactive and helpful in putting a plan together.

## 16. Bullying

The word "bully" is another of society's catch phrases that needs to be reined in. Just because a person says something that is either negative or hurtful to another, this does not label them as a bully. It becomes bullying when the same negative situation occurs over and over.

Webster's definition of a bully is: A blustering, browbeating person; one **habitually** cruel to others who are weaker; a hired ruffian.

*Side Note*: The term "*Bully*" wasn't always a negative term. In fact, President Theodore Roosevelt used to refer to the White House as the "*Bully Pulpit*", by which he meant a terrific platform from which to advocate an agenda. Roosevelt used the word bully as an adjective meaning "*superb*" or "*wonderful*", a more common usage in his time than it is today. Another expression which survives from this era is "*bully for you*", synonymous with "*good for you*". (Wikipedia)

Often times, a child becomes a bully due to their own insecurities (misery loves company). It can also stem from neighborhood drama/feuds between parents, which usually carry over to the children and into the school. Keeping that open line of communication between yourself, the student and the parents can give you the "heads up" you need to intervene before the situation gets out of hand.

The kind of bully that concerns me more than anything is the adult, specifically the teacher. Teachers can be a bully without even realizing it, which makes it all the more important to do some kind of daily reflection. We all have had that student who has made it their mission to drive us completely crazy for the first half of the year. You have called home in an attempt to involve the parents, followed your schools discipline protocols, and tried to stay positive, but to no avail. Here is where the situation can take a nasty, often unintentional, turn.

Every time that student enters your room, the hair on the back of your neck goes up and your blood begins to boil before the student even opens their mouth. As soon as they do, you keep the conversation short, to the point, and do everything possible to defuse anything that could disrupt your class. Basically, you have shut them up and shut them down. You might have maintained order, but since this has become a daily routine due to the student's past behavior, the script has flipped and you are now the bully. You've played into their hands, dropped down to a child's level of behavior, and will have no leg to stand on if you are confronted by either the parent or administrator.

By definition, a parent can also be the bully more than the child. The parent that continually blows up your phone and attempts to intimidate a teacher into adjusting their child's grade is a bully. What makes matters even more difficult is the fact that you have to see their child every day in class. Keep in mind, the child is NOT the parent. So be cautious not to take out your annoyance on the child. If the parental bullying continues, contact your administrator, discuss the situation (make sure you have a record of all conversations and calls that have taken place...*CYA*), and request a meeting with all parties involved. Don't go into the meeting on the defensive, but conduct yourself in a customer service frame of mind. Don't show your hand by allowing them to see just how irritated they have made you. Just explain that you'd like to have a meeting of the minds regarding the academic well-being of their student.

Conducting a meeting or conference with an air of concern and empathy will trump an angry confrontation any day of the week, and the winning outcome should always be on the side of the child.

**Why do kids get bullied?** Believe it or not, going after the bully isn't normally the best way to solve the problem. Training others (victims and potential victims) how to best handle bullies is ultimately the best way to stop being bullied. As odd as it sounds, the victim is often the reason they are being bullied because they decided to react to the bully's initial attack. A bully comes along and tells another student that their mother is fat (or worse), and the victim becomes angry and takes action to try and make them stop. They call them names back, yell at them, punch them in the face, tell a teacher or tell the Principal. The teasing doesn't stop and in many cases, it gets worse. The real reason the victim is getting teased is because *the victim is getting upset!* The victim is playing into the bully's hands and fueling them to continue or even step up their game. They are giving the bully exactly what they want.

***How do you stop the bully?*** Kids are terribly frightened of being a "snitch", due to peer pressure and the internet. So first, the kids need to change their attitude towards what's being said or done. Once they change the way they think about the bullying, everything else will fall into place. I know it's hard, but the victim should not react about what's being said about them. Do NOTHING. They're not to say STOP or call them names back. Don't even be angry at them. If the teaser puts their face in the victims face and says, "What's the matter, don't you hear me?" it's alright to answer, "Yes, of course I hear you!" If the victim feels they need to speak more, they can continue with, "If you want to call me names, that's OK", or, "If you enjoy making fun of me, you can do it all day long." Doing this should stop them fairly quickly as long as the victim says it without getting angry. Even if what they are saying is true, the victim should say and do nothing. It is the bully who will usually look stupid.

**\*Sales Timeout:**

Sales Professionals encounter bullies all day, every day. It is easy to get mad and upset about what is being said about us or our company, when they are just trying to get us to lower our price.

**\*Sales Timeout:**

Customer Service Professionals also get bullied a lot on the phone, more so than a Sales Professional which is a face to face confrontation. Being on the phone gives many people the courage to say rude things and beat on the innocent Customer Service Professional that is only trying to assist you. It's the company, many times, that is the one in the wrong or makes solving the problem harder that it has to be. Both the Sales and Customer Service Professional has to keep their attitude in check. They both understand that the attack isn't directed at them (in most cases). You may even see the Professionals apologize when they did nothing wrong, just to calm the aggressor down. Again, just like the kids that are getting bullied, Sales Professionals have to keep their attitudes in check and let the situation play out.

## 17. Rigor

The new magic vocabulary word of the educational world is now "Rigor". The basic definition is to have classroom expectations that encourage students to think critically, creatively and more flexibly. Over the last two years, rigor has become one of the most overused, over explained and obnoxious words in our schools, meetings and trainings. And yet, it is something that has been lacking in our schools across the country. Think about it, no one wants "Rigor Mortis" occurring in the classroom. No one enjoys trying to learn in a stiff, lifeless classroom, whether you are the teacher or a student. The lesson MUST grab, keep and enlarge the student's ability and desire to learn the topic. But, in this ever changing world of the "Me Generation", how do we do this?

Quite simply, the lesson needs to be relevant (see *Selling Education* **Hot Topic** #8) and as much about the students and their world as possible in order to keep their attention. The days of teaching a lesson just because it's part of the standards have come and gone. Sadly, if the lesson does not directly impact the student's world or particular ambition, many of them just don't care and will blow through your assignment just to get it over with. Statements like, "You will need this in the future" carry very little weight. Teachers now have the arduous task of playing Sociologist and Psychologist in order to discover each student's thoughts, dreams and desires in order to plan out their daily lessons. As early as 5 years ago, the only students with IEPs (Individual Education Plans) were in the Special Ed units. Now, in order to be successful, diverse and rigorous, *each* of our students actually needs to have such a plan. Keep it simple. Survey your students and discover their likes, dislikes, goals, etc.… Doing this quick and easy task will enlighten you to their ambitions, and help you to learn your clientele (see *Selling Education* **Hot Topic** #4), which in turn will build that needed relationship. Simply put, you cannot sell ice to an Eskimo!

## District Leaders and Politicians…Now here this!

If you demand rigor and relevance in the classroom, we can no longer have over crowded rooms with only one teacher doing the job. Successful planning for our students requires smaller class sizes that lend to academic grouping and peer teaching, co-teachers (specifically with inclusion models), and the technology our students require and deserve in order to reach their academic and lifelong goals. Let's stop talking and debating about it, and make it happen.

**\*Sales Timeout:**

Throughout sales training, potential representatives are taught through practical learning and role play to understand what can happen and what to do when approached with certain obstacles and objections. Help your staff stay invigorated on a daily basis by not only "hyping" **what** you are selling, but **why** they are selling it to customers. Again, if the Sales Professional is not excited about the product, why will the customer? You are not only their point of contact, but a direct advertisement for both the product you are trying to sell and your company.

# HOT TOPICS –
# EDUCATING SALES

## Sales Introduction by Chuck

When starting my journey into the world of Sales, I told myself that this is temporary, a stepping stone to get back into my passion of aerospace. That was before I became a Top Representative. That rush you get when being responsible for your own success, and achieving a much higher degree of satisfaction than you had ever thought possible, is something you can't get enough of. Please don't forget why you do what you do, helping the people you meet every day make the right/best choice.

As you read through this section, keep in mind that this is a quick reference guide to being successful in your chosen profession of sales, and geared towards *Business to Consumer* sales. This type of sale is fun, and very rewarding, because you have no idea what situation you're going to walk into. As in any sales industry, you're going to get a few easy sales where the customer knows exactly what they want, and are willing to move forward on the spot. However, most cases will be a variety of scenarios where you need to think very quickly on your feet and deal with situations that are often times out of your control. For example, arriving at a prospects' home, the husband is mowing the grass and the wife welcomes you by saying your products/services are not needed. Or, you pull up to the house and can hear from your car that the couple you're about to try and befriend are screaming at each other. Being able to disarm the situation, try and reschedule the appointment, and doing it all in a positive way so the appointment is not cancelled, are all things you need to learn how to overcome in order to be successful. Even though this section doesn't cover *all* situations that you will encounter during your career as a Sales Professional, it will give you a rock solid foundation to start working through these situations and not lose technique while following your company's sales processes. If you're new to sales and you learn, practice and utilize these techniques over a six month period, it will improve your performance in front of the customer and make everyone involved feel more comfortable. If you give these techniques the time and attention you and they deserve, you will perfect your ability to sell.

The reader will also see the authors refer to both students and teachers throughout the Educating Sales section. This is to assist Educators who would like to learn the sales process and strengthen their own careers in education.

Now that's out of the way, here are a couple of precursor lessons I discuss when working with new sales professionals which help them to understand how people work. These are paramount when working with young people due to their stage in life and your ability to influence their thinking.

**Perception is EVERYTHING** - A person's perception is their reality, it is their fact. If you try and change that, you are simply going to get into a struggle where you stand no more than a 10% chance of winning.

**If there is a chance you can be misunderstood, you will be** - Make sure that you are clear with what you are saying. Leave no room for misunderstanding or misinterpretation. When a new sales professional or a student says, "But I thought you meant...," YUP, that's your fault! Don't get mad at the student, you created that in the students mind by not being completely clear.

**Tellin' Ain't Sellin'** - In sales we call this "*Park and Puke.*" You may have seen this if you had a sales representative come to your home in an attempt to sell you something, and they just sit there yapping and yapping about their product or service. They never ask you what you think, or if it would even fit your needs. An hour later, the so-called "professional" is still yapping, and when he is finished you tell him, "We need to think about it" just to get him out of your house! Now you spend the rest of the day thinking about the two hours of your life you'll never get back. The next person you have out is a TRUE Sales Professional. He asks you all kinds of fact finding questions and intelligently works you towards the direction that would best suit you and your family's needs. He makes purchasing easy, is aware of your time and considers the fact that you've had a long day before he got there. When he or she also makes the visit enjoyable…SOLD! As a teacher, you need to look at this the same way. I have suffered through many high school and college courses where you can tell the teacher/ professor either just wants to get this done and over with, or simply lacks the social skills needed to teach the course effectively. SELL the kids on learning the lesson of the day! Ask them questions and get them involved, so that they aren't daydreaming or passing notes because you lost their attention 5 minutes after class started.

**Taking Control** - I do a lot of training with both new and seasoned sales professionals, and the one topic that gets everyone's interest is "How to take control." So whether your desire is to take control of a room or just a conversation, there is a very simple technique that will change the way you communicate after you try it a few times. So what is the technique you ask??? **Asking Questions**! Yep, that's it… Not as easy as you may think however. Next time you witness a conversation that you're not a part of, watch and decide who is in control of that conversation. I will bet you an ice cream cone that the winner is the person asking more questions. And if you are witnessing a master Sales Professional, he or she will maintain control through a technique called "*Reversing.*" Reversing is the ability to answer a question with a question without being condescending or annoying. (See *Selling Education* **Hot Topic** #15.)

Now, as Eric Thomas says, "Let's get in the lab and grind!"

## 1. First Impressions

You've heard time and time again that first impressions are extremely important. You may have even been told that, "you should always put your best foot forward." I will tell you that both are true. You can be the best at what you do and a bad first impression can completely discredit you before you even begin. Great first impressions come from:

- Calculated, rehearsed and disciplined *preparation*. Depending on the type of sales you've decided to dominate, you need to understand the best way to prepare yourself for the day.
    - Do you go to your customer's home or office to sell? The night before, I would map out the house and directions to make sure that the address you have is correct. NEVER be late. Are your clothes clean and pressed? Look in the mirror and ask yourself, "would I buy from me?" Do I have all needed paperwork for the day?
    - Do you make your sales mostly on the phone? Be sure that your area is clean and

ready for tomorrow before you leave for the day. Wear clothes that make you feel successful. I'm sure that even your coolest Wonder Woman or Hulk PJs won't make you feel more successful and invincible than your favorite *I am woman, hear me roar* skirt and blouse, or power tie that everyone comments on as you walk to your desk.

- A great **Pre-Shot Routine**. (a golf term) What you do to get yourself in the right frame of mind to perform at your best. We talk about this in the *Selling Education* section of this book, but it is so important that I'm going to put it in front of you again. This routine could be music or YouTube clips for the drive into work, your customer's house or office, or it could be affirmations you tell yourself before you pick up the phone to make each call. Your Pre-Shot Routine is a tune up of your attitude and motivates you to feel confident and ready for whatever comes your way.
- Focused **execution** of your plan or system.
  - **In-Home Sales** – Parking on the street when possible to make sure that you're not blocking anyone in if they have to leave. When you meet the prospect for the first time, ask if where you parked is okay. If you're talking on the phone when pulling

up to your customer's house, keep driving and finish the call down the street. Do not sit outside their home and talk on your phone for 10+ minutes. Get out of your car confidently and refrain from adjusting yourself or putting your paperwork together (which should have already been done). The customer is watching you in most cases at this point so walk tall and with a smile. Their already expecting a fight so show them you're soft and easy to get along with. Give the appearance that this is going to be fun and enjoyable. Watch what you carry with you when meeting the customer for the first time, you should only have your customer's info with you. Bringing in all of your cases and samples will tell your customer, "*Better pack a lunch; this is going to be a long night*". Knock on the door, unless a note on the door tells you to ring the doorbell. When that door open's be ready for your **entry statement**, "*Mrs. Smith? Hi, Mrs. Smith, my name is Chuck Thokey with ABC Company and I'm here for our 5:00 appointment. Thank you for inviting us to your home today. By the way, did the office explain what you could expect from us today?*" From there you would narrate

> how the appointment will go. *Dave Yoho*
> calls it their *value of the visit.*

If all this is done as you have scripted it, your first impression will have helped the customer feel more at ease with the appointment. Your goal is to set the ground work for **TRUST** to be established. Remember that if you set a bad first impression, you can come back from it. However, you're really climbing a steep hill to make up for your lack of preparation, or something you said, because you weren't scripted coming into the door.

**\*Education Timeout:**

The first impression *anyone* has of you as a professional is critical. If your administrator observes you dragging into the front door of the building, you can almost be guaranteed of an evaluative walk through sometime that morning (I would). How can you teach a rigorous lesson if you barely made it from your car to the classroom? Whether you are a teacher or in sales, your customer can and will smell indifference. Another thing you want to be cautious of doing is sharing details as to *why* you are not necessarily up to a mental par that day. Your boss, your peers, and particularly your clients/students DO NOT CARE. Keep your private life private. You are there to do a job and serve your clients. Period.

When a parent and/or student walks into your classroom at the beginning of the year, get out from behind that desk and greet them *all* with a handshake and a smile. This instantly shows the family that they are a priority, and a welcome addition to your classroom. No one wants to feel like an intrusion, especially families who are new to the school and are arriving mid-year. If you are in the middle of a lesson when they arrive, quickly ask them to come in and have a seat at either a table or even your desk, until there is a break in the lesson. Not only will the parents and new student receive a *snapshot* of your teaching style, but your current students will see that no matter who walks into the room, the lesson being taught takes priority. The same goes for Sale Professionals. If a prospective customer arrives at your office while you are concluding a sale with another customer, do not leave them waiting and *empty*. Have the waiting area in a position where they can observe you and their customer *peer*, and put relevant literature in their hand to keep them informed.

Administrators, board members, and district officials...the above statement also applies to you. If you walk in the door to observe my classroom, do not expect to be treated as anything more than a fly on the wall. I will acknowledge your presence with a nod and a smile, but I will continue on. Asking a teacher to stop "mid-lesson" is not only rude to the teacher, but disrespectful to the students who are trying to learn the lesson being presented. If you need to talk to a teacher, make an appointment.

## 2. Having a system/process

Having a preplanned, complete system or process that you work during every appointment or phone call will keep you focused on the customer. When constantly thinking about what you should do next, you're not listening to the customer. Working a system will make the appointment effortless and flow smoothly towards getting a favorable decision at the end of the call. I don't care if you have a 5, 10 or even 15 step selling system. (Ok…15 are WAY too many steps!) Learn it and practice it like your life depends on it, and I guarantee you'll be happy with your consistent positive results. A sample *in home selling process* would look something like this:

- **Preparation** – As mentioned in *First Impressions*, make sure you're ready for the appointment.
- **Entry/Warmup** – *Trust* is gained during this step. Knowing that the stage curtains open the moment you pull up to the house. Knowing your entry statement and how you're going to make the customer feel more at ease. Explain what's going to happen during the appointment so that your customer doesn't feel lost in the process. Everyone likes to see the map of the road they're traveling on.
- **Inspection** – *Credibility* comes from your ability to give a thorough inspection of the project you're there for. Many times this may include a *walk-around,* which is when you have the customer

explain their concerns and sell themselves on why they need you there. When you're doing an inspection and the customer isn't watching, a video of the inspection is vital to the *Trust* and *Credibility* you're building during the appointment. Pictures need to be taken in addition to the video so that you have a complete inspection packet to present.

- **Presentation** – A *Masterful* presentation is art. Turn the presentation that you put in front of your customer into a smooth conversation filled with engagement and education. This will be the difference between them daydreaming about what they need to do after you leave, to having a blast and buying because you made it so fun and interesting. Be sure that you are offering more than any other company the customer may have contacted. Keep your company story short. They need to know you have a story, but they truly don't care. Your company story needs to include your company's WHY they have been successful during their time in business. The primary reason to have a presentation is to answer initial *unasked* questions. Prospects may not know what to ask after you have left. What makes you different? Why should the prospect care what you have to offer? In your presentation, educate them on the industry, product and processes. Then, bring out the villain in the industry: Competition products. Show the prospective buyer that you and your company are the hero. (This is explained further in *"Story Telling"*.

- **Demo** – Have a product or service that you're able to demonstrate to the customer. A demonstration of superiority to other competitive products should be done in order to tip over the *credibility* bucket you're filling during the appointment.

- **Trial Close** – Hopefully *trust* and *credibility* has been earned and you have gotten to the point that you're ready to show the customer their investment. Going further, your goal is to make sure that if you get anything other than YES while asking for the order, it's narrowed down to money. A simple but powerful question of, *"Other than price and affordability, is there any reason you wouldn't want to move forward while I'm here?"* That question was taught to me when I started selling and it has served me and those professionals I have trained very well. Using this technique, the sales professional needs to understand why they would use it so that when objections arise, they know money is the issue. Once you discover that finances could be the issue, simply find out if it's the "**Price**" you're asking for the product, or it's "**Affordability**", which they may think won't fit into their budget. Either of those you can generally negotiate your way through and walk out with the sale.

- **Present Price** – Showing the customer their investment should always start with the retail price. Let it sink in before presenting any discounts your company may offer. Generally, you will have 3 prices to give to a customer. Your retail price which can be good for 12 months, your discounted pricing that is good for 30 days, and then a price that allows you and your company to save money through time and efficiency. This is an incentive to move forward while you're at the house. Be sure to justify your pricing by showing the value in your product or service. Remember how much it costs you to continue to come back several times, and miss out on seeing another prospect that needs your help.

- **Close** – We hear so often that this is the most sought after skill for a sales professional. Yes, you do need to know how to ask for the order, and what to say if they hand you objections/excuses. However, a majority of the calls you run can be sold without any issues if you understand the strong closing method I was taught very early in my career. The closing method is called *The Goodnight Kiss Close*, by Ben Gay III, The Closers. For you men out there, go back to when you were in college and you took a girl on a date. When bringing her back home, what could you do right then to guarantee a goodnight kiss? Give up? The answer is NOTHING. Its *"everything"* you did throughout the night that puts you in a good position to get a kiss at the end of the evening.

Opening the door for her, paying for her meal, etc. It works the same way in sales. You can't skip all of the other steps of the sale or even *kind of* do them. The sales professional needs to be fully invested in each step of the selling process so that when it comes to asking for the order, a YES is the natural conclusion of the appointment. Closing is a skill that needs to only be used on difficult customers, or when you may have missed something and the customer just isn't sold yet.

- **Button-up** – After you have closed the deal, a small number of customers may get a disease call *Buyer's Remorse*. This disease tends to show up after the cool down period, typically within 24 to 48 hours. I like to tell my sales professionals that after you have closed the sale, *cuddle* (mentally) with the customer to make sure that there are no signs of them canceling after you have left the home. I have seen many sales professionals simply ask about them canceling. *"So Tom and Mary, every now and again after I leave a customer's home, they think about the money they just spent and call to cancel the order. Is there any reason you can think of that you would need to cancel?"* This is very strong, especially once the customer confirms that they can't think of any reason that would need to cancel. So now you have their commitment to do business, and you have also gotten their commitment not to cancel.

Don't allow this to be your last contact with the customer. Make sure that you follow up on how the install/service went and if you could come out to look at it and take pictures. When you meet with the customer again, be sure to talk about keeping you in mind for other projects or future needs. Ask if they know of any current needs a friend or family member may have, and ask permission to make contact with them. If the friend or family member does business with you, offer the original customer an incentive.

**\*Education Timeout:**

Just like any customer, students need to feel the comfort level of consistency, daily procedures, the importance of the product being sold, and reliability of the person *selling* the information to them.

As stated in *Selling Education* Hot Topic 2, Setting up for Success, it is critical to be prepared for the new school year. I have seen SO many teachers walk in the door after enjoying their summer time off (which is well deserved), and begin attempting to plan for the year during those 2-3 days before students arrive. This is a recipe for disaster. About a month before school begins, sit down and do the following two things:

1. Prepare at least 2 weeks of lessons and activities for your students. Yes, you may have to alter a few things with possible schedule changes that could occur within the building over the summer, but the basic plan is there. If your school opens early, go in and make any needed copies for your students in order to kill off that tedious, necessary evil.

2. Write out an outline of the district, school, and classroom rules and procedures that your students will need to know. Put them on a clipboard and have them ready to go for Day One. I don't care how long you've been in education; don't try to go through your processes *on the fly*. Day One is historically hectic and interruptive, so you will forget something unless you plan in advance.

Now, when you arrive at your building to begin the new school year, the priorities will be: room set up, student lists, pre-year meetings and professional developments. Completing steps 1 and 2 above before you walk into the school will give you that necessary breathing room needed to survive.

## 3. Teams

It is extremely important in the sales world that we promote a TEAM environment. When a sales professional is out on their own island, they can only have a certain amount of success before they level off and struggle to gain any more momentum. As new sales professionals join the team, they will encounter a system we call *"Accountibilibuddy"*, where each rep is paired with another whose strengths are the others weaknesses. These reps are paired for 3 months and points are gained by improvements made. Why does this benefit a new sales professional? The new person is paired with Top Reps that are excellent communicators and have a passion of helping others succeed. The success of the Accountibilibuddy program is off the charts when done correctly and measured often.

**\*Education Timeout:**

One of the most extreme stressors in the world is either being a new student in a new school, or a new company employee. It is the teacher or managers job to alleviate that stress. Whether you are a young child trying to fit it, or new sales professionals with the desire to prove yourselves, you need to know where you are in the pecking order. Introducing yourself and your students or staff to each other is a little time consuming, but invaluable. There are a million different ways to do this, but my favorite for students is this. Split the group into pairs (I like to pull names on Popsicle sticks so that they do not instantly pair with friends that they've known since Kindergarten) and give a 5 to 6 question survey for them to ask each other and discuss. If at all possible, include yourself in this process. Keep the questions simple, but specific (Hobbies, summer activities, expectations for the year, and so forth.) When the questionnaire is completed and the discussions die down (approx. 5-10 min.), have each student introduce the other to the class. Although many of your students know each other, and may have known each other for years, most are usually surprised by one or more of the answers given. It can often break up cliques and form new acquaintances and friendships when they realize what they have in common with someone they've never taken the time to get to know. Remember to keep the cards and do this again when a new student arrives. Have your students read their own questionnaires, but have one current student survey the new student, and then introduce them to the class. Yes, this is time consuming. But, is an extremely valuable ice breaker for all involved.

If you pair students up, be sure that it is you who is doing the "pairing". Students will gravitate to those they know and, according to playground rules, someone will be left behind. Make incentives for the most improved pairings, and measure the success as often as you can. I would put this in place for 1 month, but talk to each student individually on a weekly basis to be sure that one person isn't carrying all the weight. This is great for high school students. Send home a letter for the parents so they are aware that the pairs can work on homework together, and can hold each other accountable for completing assignments.

As for sales professionals and also new teachers who join a district mid-year, up front introductions to staff that will be daily/direct contacts are imperative. Once they are acclimated, an after work *meet and greet* either in office or at the local watering hole is a great way to finish breaking the ice and introduce staff to those who only occasionally cross their paths during the work day.

## 4. Tell a story

A great story teller is a great sales professional. People love to be told a good story. Stories help the customer connect with you on a whole new level so that you can achieve the level of *trust* that only a professional like yourself could reach. Whether you're on the phone or sitting in front of them at their kitchen table, lead the customer by using a technique I call *"Walking the Dog."* My dog's name is Cooper, he's a very stubborn Siberian Husky that screams during his walks. The problem is that he either pulls you or you have to pull him. You would be happy to know that he is best dog you could ever have when he isn't being walked on a leash. When I am walking him and he wants to be stubborn, I have to gracefully and enthusiastically encourage him to continue to walk forward towards our destination. *Walking the dog* helps to prevent your customer from coming at you with *Fight or Flight* responses, and keeps them more engaged and connected with the point you're trying to make.

What is *Fight or Flight*? This is a situation where the customer, or even the Sales Rep, decides to become confrontational and start an argument. This is a *Fight* response, which leads to nothing good. When a customer has had enough and enters into a *Flight* response, they will either leave or kick the Sales Rep out of their home or office.

When you watch your favorite movie or read your favorite book, you may notice that they set the stage first. This is completed when giving a great Entry and warm-up. From here you follow just a few rules to remember:

- **Talk about the Problem first** – Sounds like common sense, but I have been out with too many sales professionals that jump right into how great their company or product is. Until the customer understands the issues, they don't care about you or your product. When starting your story the villain always comes out first, then the hero arrives. I'm sure you've never seen a movie where the white knight saves the day, and then the villain or problem arises. If you're in home improvement and you're explaining the process of doing business, you may start with how the industry works and some of the issues that the "typical" company in your industry commonly addresses.

- **Everyone loves a good Hero** - After you have the customer feeling a little insecure with the process that everyone else follows, you bring in the hero that saves the day, which would be you or your company's product/service. You solve the problem and do it by slowly explaining how you will do things differently and to the customer's benefit.

- **Your story has to come to a CLOSE** – The conclusion of your story has to be confirmed with closing them on the idea and making sure they listened and agree with your point. *"With that being said Mrs. Customer, which way would you rather do business?"* Once they give you the answer, ask them WHY? This is asking them to repeat the strong point of your product or service…selling themselves.

**\*Education Timeout:**

Story telling is ESSENTIAL to both Sales Professionals and Educators. People, no matter the age, usually love to hear about how the subject you're teaching or the item you're selling will not only impact them, but how it also impacted you. Just keep it short, to the point, and give time for a response. It is human nature for your audience to listen with one ear, and at the same time, have a story of their own sitting on the back burner before you have even finished yours. Be patient, acknowledge the relevance of both stories, know when to (politely) end "story telling time", and get back to the topic at hand.

Be truthful. It is tempting to either fabricate or borrow a story in order to pull in your audience. But, with the internet and even word of mouth, discovery of such *untruths* can completely destroy the credibility of both you and your profession. If the story is not factual and/or cannot be validated, don't use it.

## 5. Helping the customer sell themselves

You can sell more by selling less. Don't look at our book like that, I'm serious. Understand how to help the customer sell themselves and your job will become so much easier. No, this isn't a mind trick or deceptive in any way. And, I'm not telling you anything new when I say that people hate to be sold, but they love to buy. Through strategic and easy questions, you can get the customer to share with you as to why they need your product over anyone else's. Here are some example questions:

- What are your concerns?
- You've gone this long without fixing the issue, what makes you want to take care of it now?
- How does that make you feel?
- What about this issue concerns you most?
- How have you tried to fix the problem before now?
- What do you see as a solution to the problem?

Follow-up questions help you dig deeper and close a customer on the point you're making. The easiest and most powerful follow-up question is simply "Why?" When you finish your story and the customer claims you're the only way to go, or your product is the product for them, ask them *"do you mind if I ask you why?"* They should then repeat some of the main points to the story *you* just finished telling them. When you say it, you're selling *them*. However, when the customer says it, it's a fact. So again, get them to repeat your main points and *why* they are important to them. You now have just made the strongest sale possible.

**\*Education Timeout:**

Human beings require understanding of what they are purchasing, and how it is relevant to their needs (see *Selling Education* **Hot Topic** #8), before they will have complete *buy in*. Requiring an elementary student to comprehend addition and subtraction of decimals before they understand place value and money, is comparable to opening a snow removal company during the month of May in Kentucky. It will be necessary in the near future, but no one will understand why you're presenting it to them now. (Cart before the horse syndrome)

Basically, if what you're teaching/selling meets the needs of the student/client, sales now becomes a form of *customer service*. Less time is spent on the WHY should I buy, and more is spent on HOW it will benefit them.

## 6. Closing techniques

Know that you provide the best product and service in your industry. If you don't sell them, someone else will sell them something inferior, which will cost the customer more money in the long term. Your job is to protect the customer by not running out of techniques during a time when Mr. & Mrs. Customer are only thinking about the money they're spending, and not the total long term cost to themselves and their family.

The use of closing techniques are needed when the customer just hasn't heard enough to make a buying decision or has made up their mind that they aren't buying anything at this time. We will go through a few of the best "soft" closing tools used by in-home sales professionals today. First, we need to understand how to handle an objection. This goes back to "*walking the dog.*" You can't ask, "I just spent two hours with you, explaining why you need this product or service, what's your problem?" Or "What do you need to think about?" These responses lead to *Fight or Flight* reactions from the customer. They will kick you out of their home or get angry and continue to argue with you, neither of which leads to a positive outcome. Overcoming any objection takes an ability to control your emotions. I teach the **4 C's** of handling objections, I've been taught many different ways handling objections that are all the same, just different ways to remember the process.

- **Concede** - Disarming the customer is extremely important if you intend on having them listen to you and walking them down a path that allows them to see things your way. Starting with: "I understand" or "I agree," will enable you to step into their shoes and show them that you care about their concerns. Remember that the customer is expecting a confrontation, they may even be nervous telling you their objection depending on their personality. Stepping on their side of the table and letting them know that you understand and that you may even agree with their way of thinking will bring the customer's guard down enough for you to show them why they can be comfortable moving forward with you.

- **Commit** - Once you have disarmed the customer, make sure to get their commitment that the objection is the only concern they have before moving forward. You don't want to get past this objection just to face four more right after. You may find that you can squash several objections at once.

- **Convince** - Now that you have lowered their guard and brought all concerns into the spot light, you can convince the customer of the solutions to their objections. Help them to understand how you're going to handle their issues. Brian Tracy's oldie but goodie, "If I could, would you?" works here on certain objections. Example: If the objection is timing, "If I could move up the install by 2 weeks, would you move forward with the work order while I'm here?" This is a very strong negotiating technique.

- **Close** - Ensure that the customer understands your solution and that they're satisfied. With your explanation, this can be as easy as asking "Fair enough?" or "Does that answer your questions?"

Let's look at several of the most popular objections you will encounter. These objections, like most objections, are brought up after the customer's investment has been presented. Our strategies for handling these objections are based on our **Trial Close**. Remember that it allowed me to narrow everything down to MONEY. I can't just ask them about the money unless they bring it up, as it would create confrontation. So, I use the 4 C's to take their original objection *back to MONEY*.

- *"We need to think about it."* - If you're in any type of sales, your success lies heavily on your ability to handle this objection. 80% of the customers that give you this objection simply want to get out of making a decision, and get you out of their house. The problem is that many of them won't make a decision at all if you leave. Others may use a competitor that will offer them the cheap option which will cost them more in the future than if they would have spent a few more dollars with you (and had long term peace of mind). The other 20% that use this objection are "Thinkers," these customers are generally accountants, engineers, professors, etc. They truly do have to think about their decision by going through a process of dissecting the pros and cons, and coming up with their own reasons for buying. The best way to sell these customers is to give them an abundance of information on both your product and the other products they may be looking for. For the 80% that are simply trying to get out of making a decision, here is how to funnel them to money:

- ○ *I totally understand.* This is a big decision. How long do you feel you need to think about it? (Customer: "We need until next Monday.") Wow, you really are serious about getting this done aren't you? (Customer: "Yes.") Well it sounds like "System A" is the best option for your family, wouldn't you agree? And, are we the company you *trust* to install that product? (Customer: "Yes, Absolutely.") Great, so is it safe to say that it's coming down to money? (Customer: "Um, Yes it is.")

- *"I need to talk to my friend/uncle/dad/ etc...."* This is normally a delay, but again we need to bring this down to money. This objection is something that should have been brought up during the initial conversation when you got to the house, to make sure that everyone involved with the decision was present. If you forgot to bring up the additional decision makers, here is a good way to bring the objection to money:
  - ○ **That's understandable.** I have a number of friends and family that call me when making a decision like this also. Can we get your friend on the phone to include him in the information I'm providing? That way

you don't have to remember all the benefits to the product you're wanting. (Customer: "No, he is at work and can't receive calls right now.") OK, no problem. Let me ask you, how do you personally feel about spending $6,925 on this? Very important to wait for their answer. When they come back with "Well it is more than I expected." You have just eliminated their imaginary friend and are back to working with money.

- *"I need to talk to my son."* You may be thinking to yourself, why is this any different than the last objection? This objection is normally true; it usually comes from an older single individual.

    ○ **No problem Mary, can we get him on the phone?** (Customer: "No.") My mother calls me on most home improvement decisions also. I always ask her the same 3 questions (ask the questions and wait for them to respond): First question I ask is, does the product you're looking at fix the problem? (Customer: "Yes, it does.") Next, do you trust the company and the representative to do a good job? (Customer: "Yes, of course.") And can you afford it?

Make sure to wait for an answer. Many times your customer will move forward by saying, "You're right, I can make this decision and yes, I can afford it." You're going to want to button this sale up in a different way. The issue with this is often the son or daughter calling and yelling at you about selling his mother something "they feel" she doesn't need. This is why we try to get them involved. Your button up for this objection is: "Mary, now that we have everything into production and they should be calling you in a few weeks to start the work, I need to ask you something. When you call your son to tell him what you have just done, what do you think he is going to say? Getting this answer will help her with how she is going to approach her kids and keep the potential cancel from happening.

**\*Education Timeout:**

Teachers, almost all of the techniques named above are usable in the classroom. So, without being redundant, I would just like to state the following...

Time constraints during the day are a constant battle. In order to get through a lesson, teachers have a habit of jumping in as soon as their students sit down, present the lesson, give students time to work either individually or in groups, collect the classwork, assign homework and send them on their way. There is no *close* to the lesson. Do yourself and your students a favor and make time for them to either complete an Exit Ticket (one question regarding that day's lesson that is turned in as they leave the room), or Bell Work as they enter the classroom (again, one question, but based on the previous day's lesson). Not only is this a way to close out and prepare them for the next lesson, but it also gives the teacher an informal way to assess and monitor student progress.

On a personal note (as a teacher, a previous sales pro, and a potential customer), take care to sound *natural* in your sales pitch and especially, your closing. Nothing turns a potential buyer off more than talking to someone, either on the phone or in person, who sounds as if they are reading from a script. Almost everything we do in both teaching and sales is scripted. The magic happens when you can put it into your own words and humanize what you're selling.

## 7. Money Clarification

A major "elephant in the room" when it comes to selling your product is cost/money. Take the objection of *money* out of the equation through money clarification. My experience shows that when the issue is money, it's either *Value*, where the customer doesn't see paying what we're asking. Or its *affordability*, it just doesn't fit in your budget. Which one is it for you?

- **Affordability** – (*Customer: "Yeah, it just doesn't fit in our budget right now."*) *Is it the Monthly Payment or the Down Payment that's giving you a problem?* Depending on your company, you should be able to alter either one that the customer has an issue with. But before you do alter anything to get the job, you need to get a commitment from the customer stating that if you get approval to alter their deal, they will move forward. *So, if I was able to obtain a longer term of the financing, you would move forward?, or So, what could you put down today? (Customer: "$1500.00") Wow, that is quite a bit less. I'm not sure I can get an approval for that amount, but if I could…you would move forward?*
- **Value** – Ask the customer what they thought the price would be before you came out. Then go back over the benefits and differences to your product and ask them where they are on price now. Hopefully they see the value and come up

closer to where you are. From here, you're going to want to break the job down to the ridiculous by showing them that it will actually cost them just a few dollars per day to own your product.

**\*Education Timeout:**

Without proof of relevance and need, anyone selling a product is fighting an uphill battle. Seems to be a continuous pattern here, right? Educationally, there are obvious costs for parents. Some are non-negotiable, such as school levies that impact property taxes. Others, dependent on income levels, can be subsidized by individual state programs (free breakfast/lunch, books, supplies, and so forth). When it comes to my students, I do everything I can to show them that they can't afford *not* to buy into their education. It just takes time, and it's FREE! The value comes from taking what you've learned and finding a way to apply it to your life in order to better yourself not only financially, but personally. Very few people in this world are NOT looking for a better way of life. Unless you win the lottery, education in any way, shape, or form is the first step towards meeting that goal.

## 8. When in a slump

After you read *Selling Education and Educating Sales,* and structure it for your company and industry, I know you'll be more successful than you thought possible. However, over time you'll start altering your technique and dropping steps of the sale. Just like a car, once so many parts have fallen off, it will stop running. This is how slumps occur, even the best sales professionals adjust their technique so much over time that they have to stop and relearn what they were taught when they started selling. When you want to know what you're not doing, hit your reset button and go back to the beginning.

- *Quick Sand* – "The Replacements" (starring Keanu Reeves and Gene Hackman) are a team of supposed wannabe NFL players living their dream of playing professional football during a players strike. There is a scene where Gene Hackman asks the players at half time about their biggest fear. Several of the players give fears that have nothing to do with the game (spiders, for example), but Keanu Reeves character, Shane Falco, mentions *Quick Sand*. He explains it as making a mistake, and then another mistake, then another until you are in so deep that it feels as if you are swimming in quick sand and can't get your head back into the game. As sales professionals, our quick sand consists of head trash, trimming off steps of the sale, and our attitude. Once we have lost numerous techniques from not using them like we should, we start to miss sales, which will lead to quick sand. You lose your momentum and your month goes into the proverbial toilet.

- *Why new sales reps rise to the top quickly* - There is a reason why many new reps often perform better and sell more than your veteran sales professionals. They know the basics and haven't learned all the bad habits that the veterans have picked up over the years. Some call this a *"Dummy Curve"* where the reps just don't know how to mess up yet. I've even heard it called *"Beginners Luck"* which is laughable, because all sales are mixed with very little luck and a lot of attitude and training. When you begin with a company that concentrates on a two to three week training program, your skill bucket is filled with everything you'll need to be a Top Sales Professional. When your skill bucket is full and you have the right attitude, you're unstoppable!

- *Commission Breath* – Don't worry, I'm not asking you to brush your teeth. Even though it's a good idea to brush your teeth regularly, I'm talking about the moment you're in need of money and the prospect can sense it easily. Having had many sales people try and sell me goods and services over the years, I don't have to be a sales guru to easily know which of those sales professionals needed that sale to pay their mortgage or car payment. These are the people that came into my house with a hypothetical *"closing bat"*. They're rude and extremely pushy. Not taking **NO** for an answer is something I expect in a good sales professional, but to insult me or get upset because I didn't purchase their product or service is simply inexcusable. The best sales professionals I have had the pleasure of training and working with understand *Emotional Intelligence* to the level of mastery. I highly recommend getting *Emotional Intelligence 2.0* from Talent Tree and taking the exam that comes with it. Emotional Intelligence covers every aspect of your emotions as well as helping you to understand the emotions of those around you. During a time that you're in a slump or simply being told NO during your closing process, understanding how to control your own emotions can save the deal, or at least cause a customer to call you back after your competitor goes in and loses his or her temper.

Finally, as a Sales Manager, it is imperative to know how to get sales professionals back on their feet after they have fallen into a slump.

- First, the Manager needs to sense when a sales rep is falling into a slump in order to minimize the damage.
- Have the rep ride with others that are doing well. You riding with him and pointing out what he or she is supposedly doing wrong will do nothing but make them feel worse. Watching another rep that is selling can help bring his attitude back to a more positive and motivated state.

- Then, have the suffering rep in to talk with you about what he observed during his ride. I don't want him to tell me what he thinks he is doing wrong yet, for he needs to understand everything from the successful reps attitude, to the prospects attitude to the steps of the sale.
- For the next 4 weeks you'll want to bring the rep in to practice, practice and practice again.

**\*Final Education Timeout:**

And being in a slump is one of the reasons why I desired to write *Selling Education and Educating Sales*. We've all been there, whether you are a first year teacher, or been in education for over 30 years. It happens. Slumps can happen when it comes to individual students, a particular class, parents, peers, administrators, politicians or in the eyes of the general public.

Personally delving into this project was not only to assist aspiring new Teachers and Sales Professionals jump off to a productive start, but also to let those who are seasoned and struggling know that they are not alone. There can be a light at the end of a sometimes dark and thankless rainbow. No one likes to fail, but failure is a way of life if you are constantly trying to better yourself and the profession you chose. You just have to choose the best way to pull yourself up, dust yourself off, and move forward towards the betterment of you and whatever client you serve.

As both an Educator and past Sales Professional, I have personally read numerous *self-help* books that claim to be the salvation of our professions. Most state the same rhetoric, change an adjective or adverb here and there in order to make it "new", and come after our money. The inspiration for *Selling Education and Educating Sales* came from personal experiences and the needs of my peers. I firmly believe that if I glean two or three ideas from a book that will benefit me and/or my students, it was well worth the time and money. My hope is that you have found something within these pages which will benefit you.

# THE 10 DISCIPLINES OF A SUCCESSFUL EDUCATOR AND SALES PROFESSIONAL

1. *Accepting Total Responsibility for Results* - Success is in "your" hands.
2. *A Commitment to Excellence* - Thinking outside the box.
3. *An "Expectant "Attitude* - Expect to succeed everyday with your students or clients.
4. *Establish Goals* - In accordance with effective goal setting techniques.
5. *A Specific Plan of Action* -A goal without a plan is like a destination without a map.
6. *A Commitment to Yourself* - The successful educator is eager to work all resources.
7. *Insulation from the Common Teachers Cold... Negativity* - Maintain a positive attitude as much as humanly possible.
8. *Flexibility in Thinking* - Acceptance of new ideas.
9. *Maximize Creativity* - Doing what it takes every day to increase effectiveness
10. *Belief* - Believe in yourself, your students, your school, your customers and your effort. If you don't believe, no one else will either.

# SELF-ESTEEM

**The SECRET to success....** This is the most googled phrase in America today. I'd like to now share with you what so many successful professionals know and use to **WIN** every time. More importantly, it has been monumental in helping kids and young adults take control of their **Self-Esteem**. The secret is in an old sales technique that has made many sales pros very wealthy. It's called "Identity/Role", a term made popular by the *Sandler Sales Institute*.

Your **IDENTITY** = How *YOU* see *YOURSELF*. Every day when you leave the house, you position yourself from 1-10. You can see yourself as a champion "10" or totally worthless "1".

Your **ROLE** = How *EVERYONE ELSE* sees *YOU*. Whether you're playing a sport, working out, taking a test, asking someone out on a date or selling something; you lead the way with your ROLE. Just like your Identity, people see you from 1-10 with 10 being that you're the person they want to date, do business with or pick for starter of the game!

Here is where the rubber meets the road, "Your **ROLE** can never be higher than your **IDENTITY**." Seeing yourself (Your Identity) as a 5, your Role (How everyone else sees you) CANNOT be higher than a 5.

Again, if you wake up, knock the alarm off the nightstand, hit your toe on the way to the bathroom, and tell yourself you just need to go back to bed because that's how your day is going to go, you may have placed yourself at a 4. So unless you take a few minutes to increase your self-awareness and raise your Identity, people will see you as a 4 throughout the day. You will see people turn away from you, disregard you and may even see you as an easy target for getting bullied.

When is a good time to start teaching your youth about Identity / Role? As kids go into Middle School, it is necessary they understand the importance of Self-Esteem.

(Self-Esteem = Your Identity + Your Understanding that it's okay to Fail)

Helping your students, your staff, or even your own child with how they see themselves affects their performance in school as well as their influence on their friends and peers. Helping them understand that it's okay to FAIL, and most likely will FAIL through the years, will *"Bullet Proof"* their Self-Esteem.

*Selling Education and Educating Sales* has been proudly written **by** a Teacher and Sales Professional **FOR** Teachers and Sales Professionals.

# ABOUT THE AUTHORS

*Brian L. Gross is currently an elementary mathematics teacher in Dayton, Ohio. After graduating from Miami University in 1990 with a B.S. in Elementary Education, he acquired marketing, sales and banking positions with job  descriptions ranging from customer service, collections, loan officer, branch liaison and sales manager. When the banking industry began its downward slide, he returned to the classroom and has been teaching for the past 11 years. Brian currently lives in Miamisburg, Ohio, with his wife and two daughters.

*Chuck Thokey has been managing and training top sales talent for over 10 years, and has been a top ranking sales professional himself. Chuck was diagnosed with a severe learning disability in Middle School, making his ability to understand math problems or reading a book very difficult. Having a drive to succeed against all odds, Chuck graduated high school and went on to be one of the youngest Functional Test Engineers in the aerospace industry. Chuck also speaks to area schools and colleges about climbing your way to success no matter what is holding you back. He has a wife and four children living in Kettering, Ohio. Please visit Chuck's webpage at <u>www.ChuckInspires.com.</u>

Printed in the United States
By Bookmasters